Cute Girls

GRAYSCALE COLORING BOOK FOR ADULTS

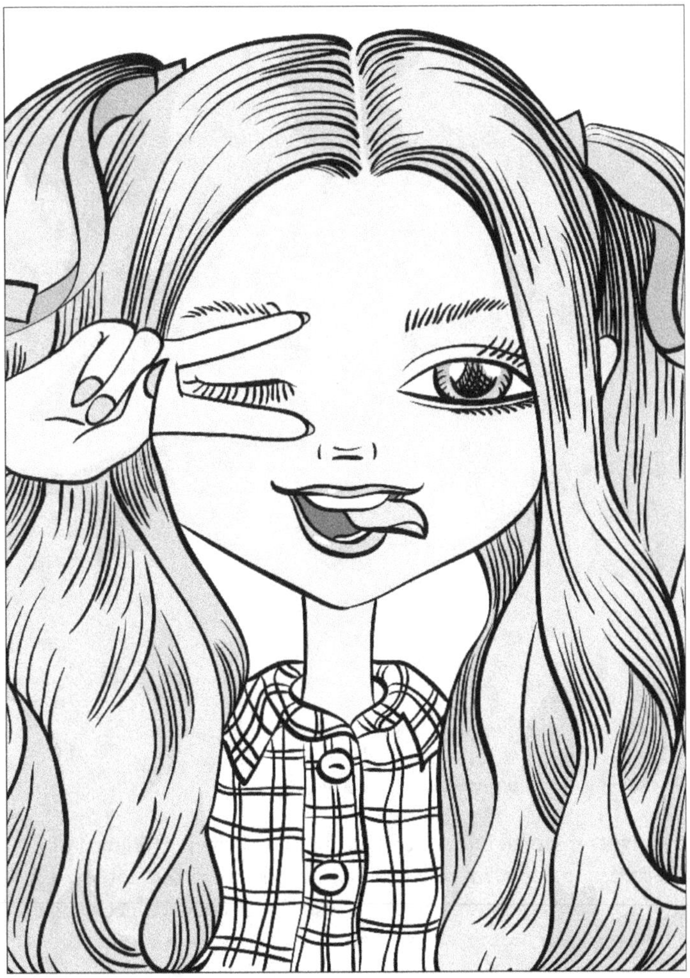

Majestic COLORING

www.MajesticColoring.com

ISBN: 978-1548253097

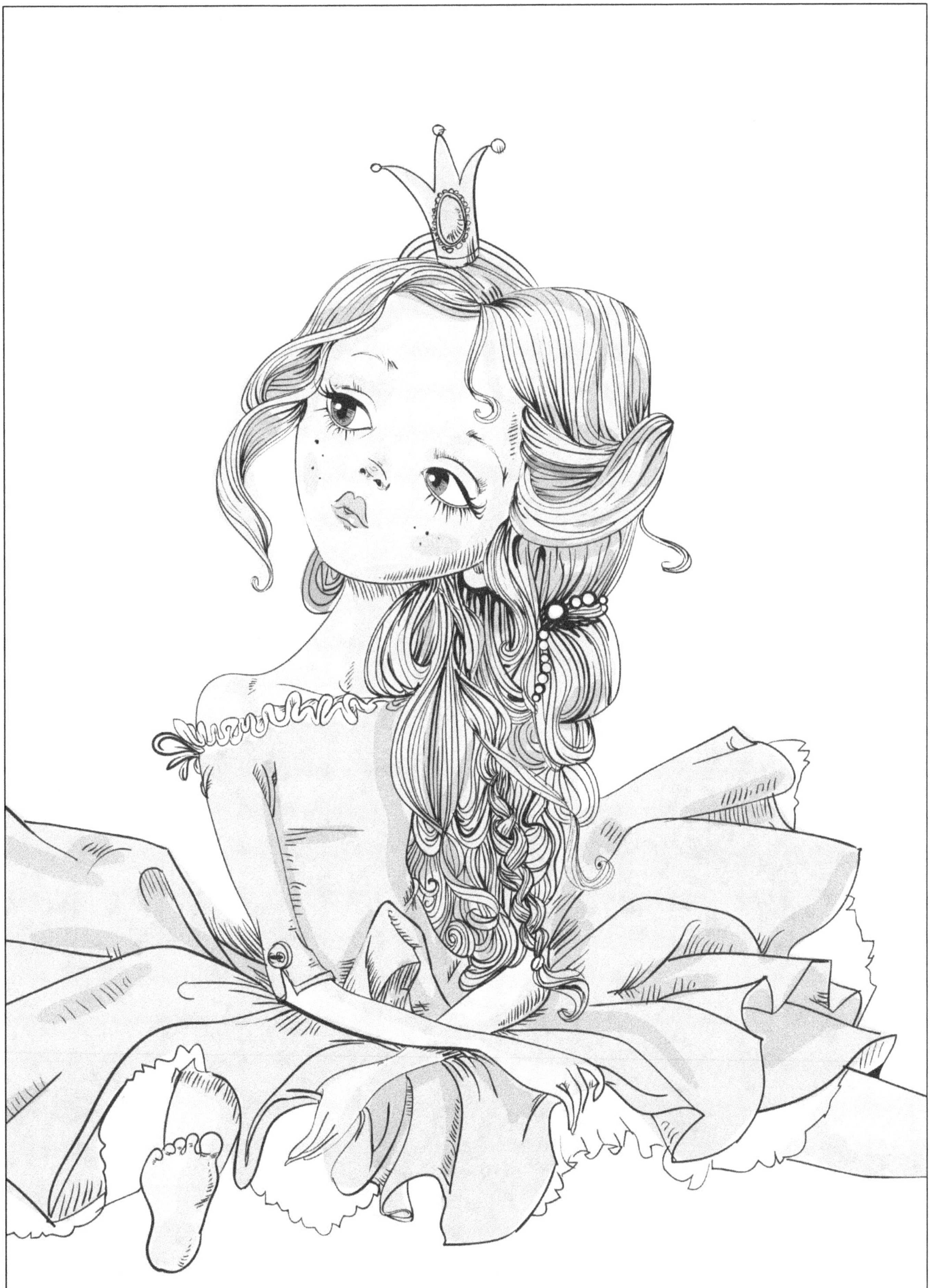

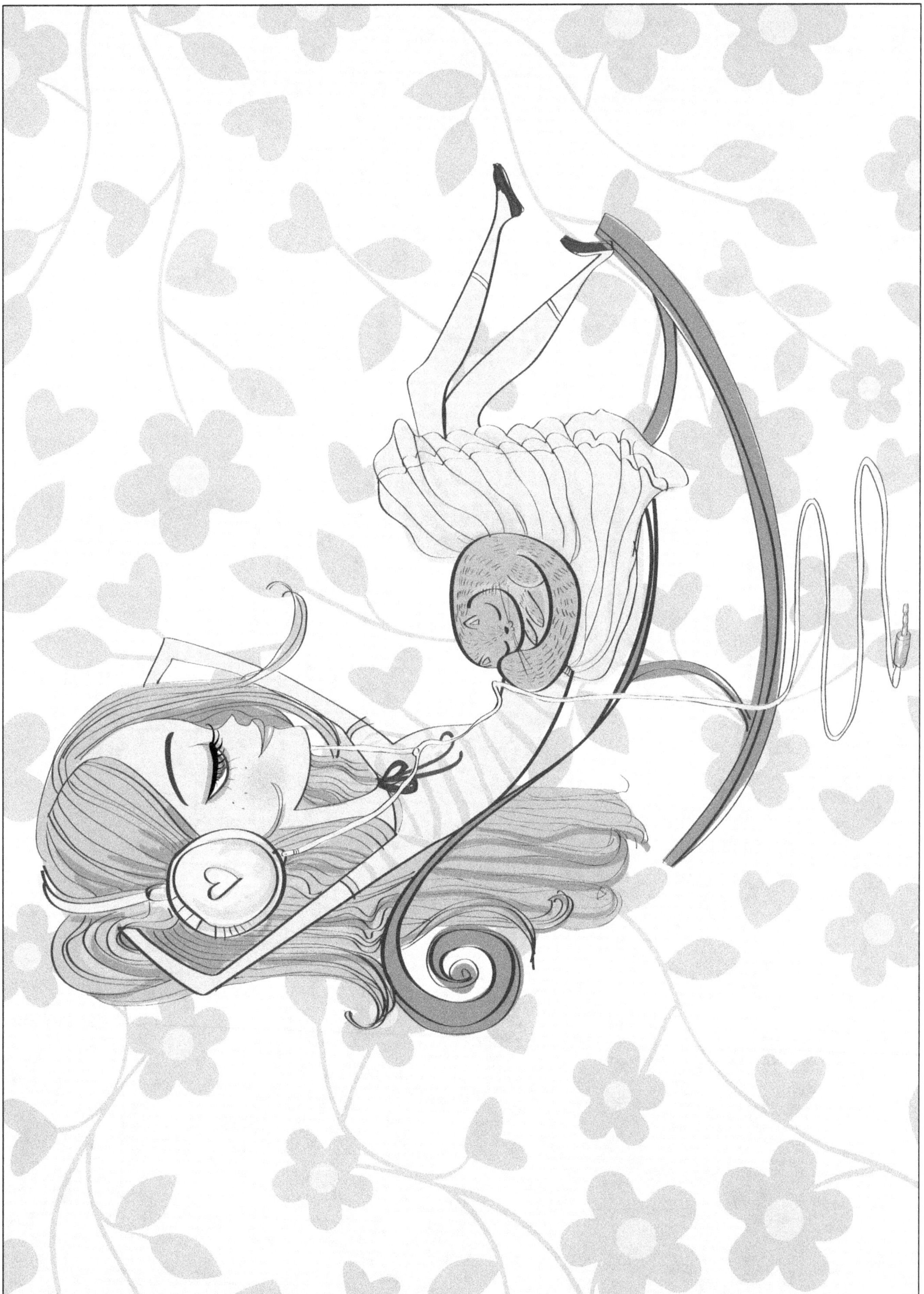

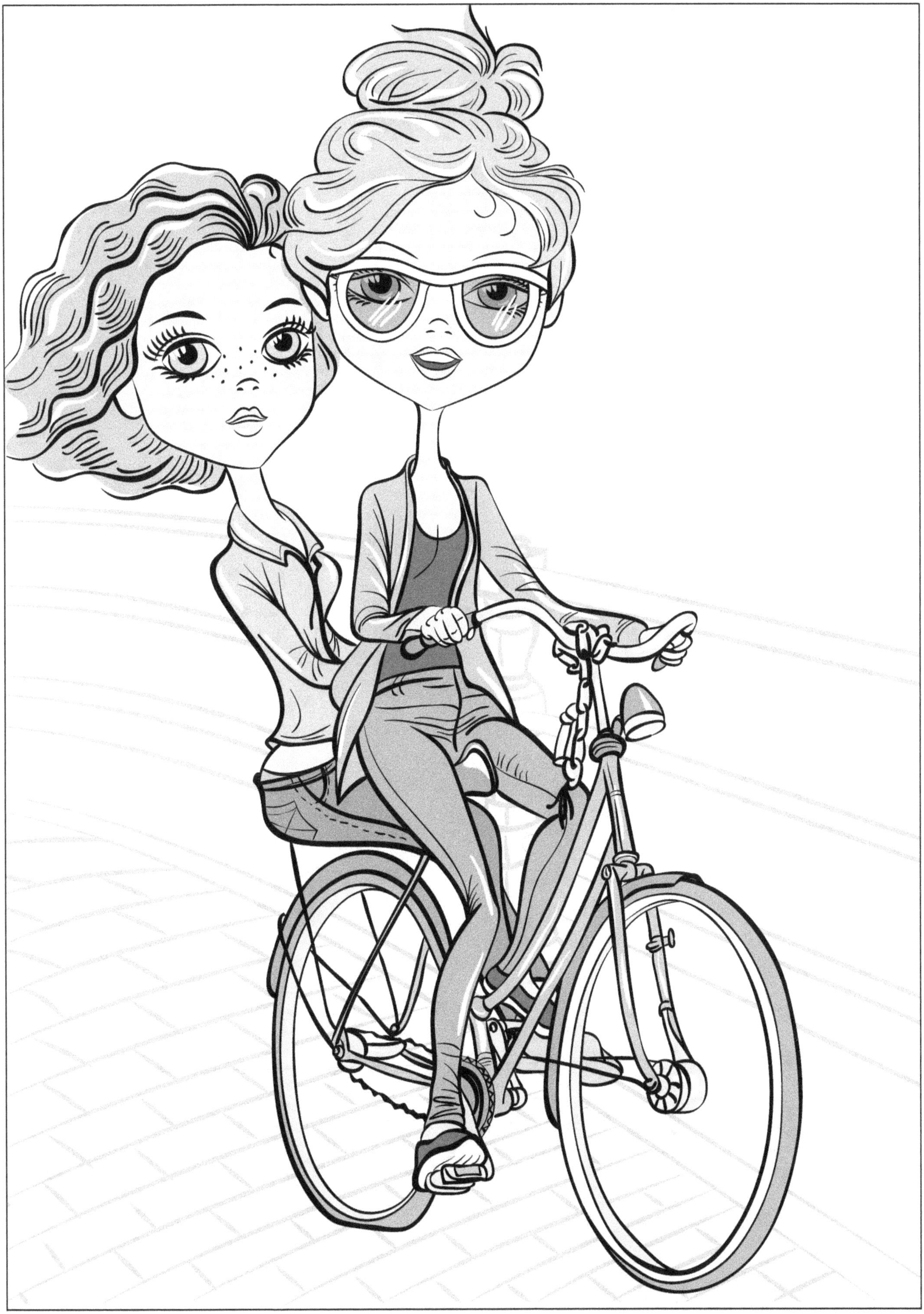

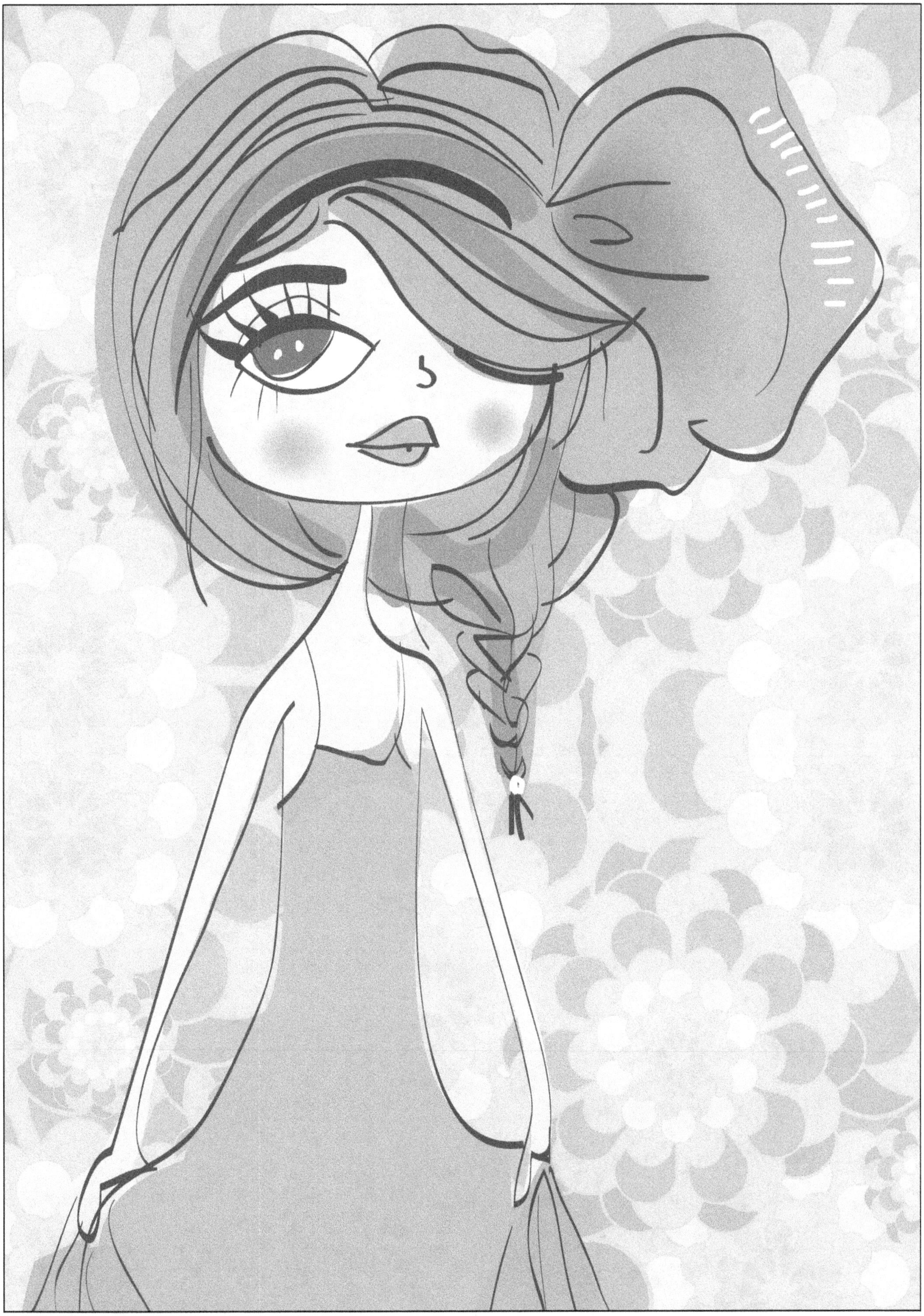

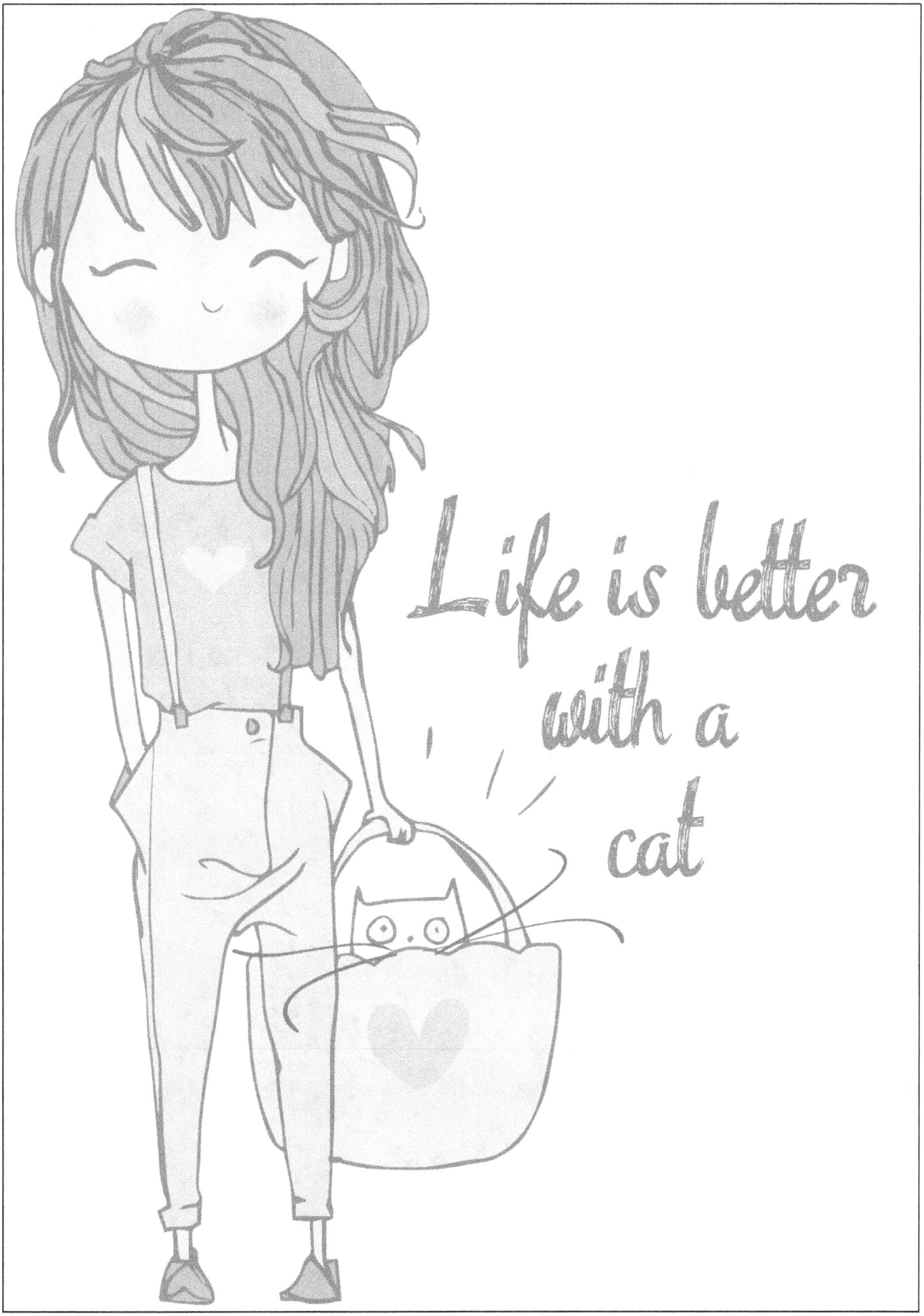
Life is better
with a
cat

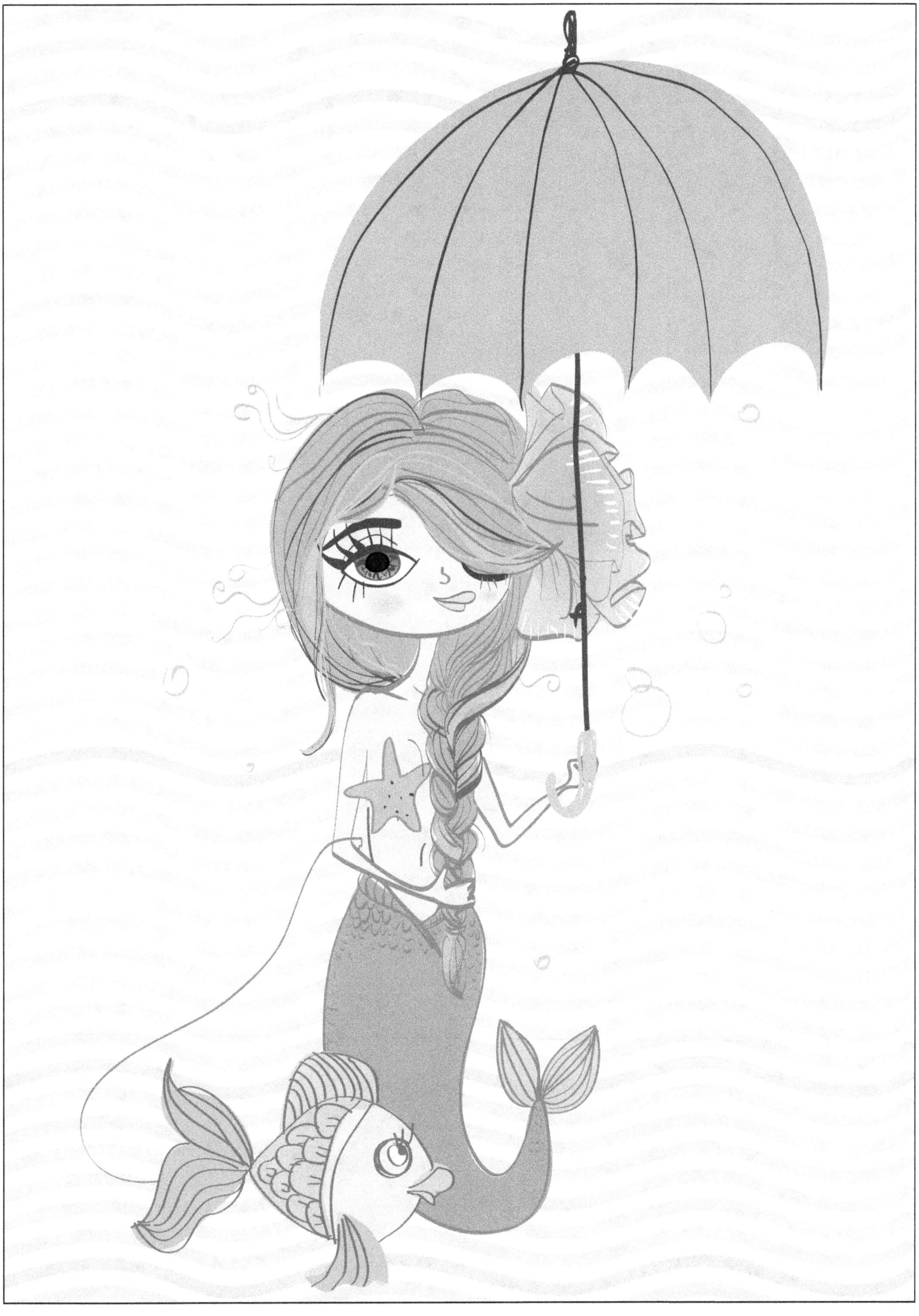

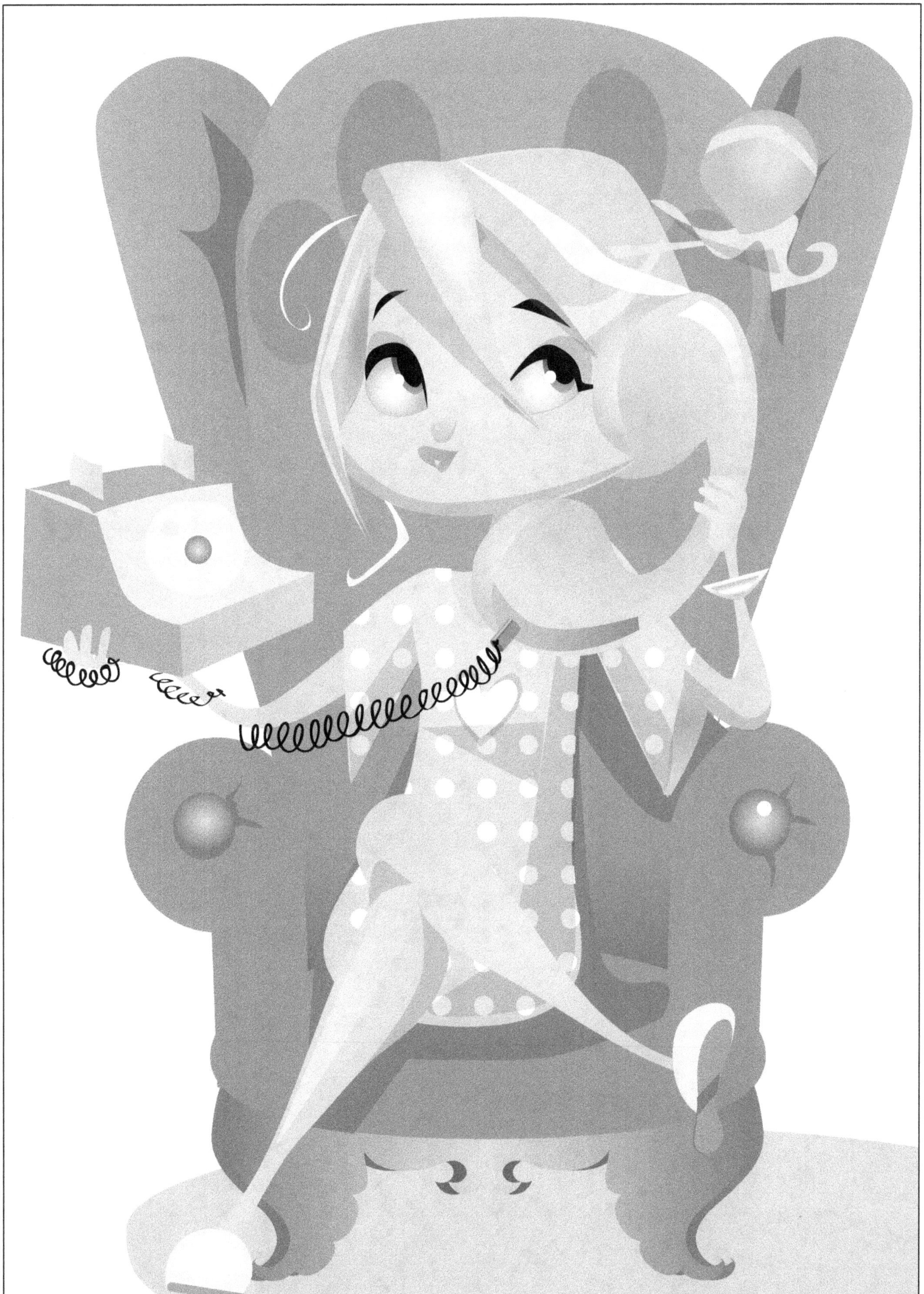

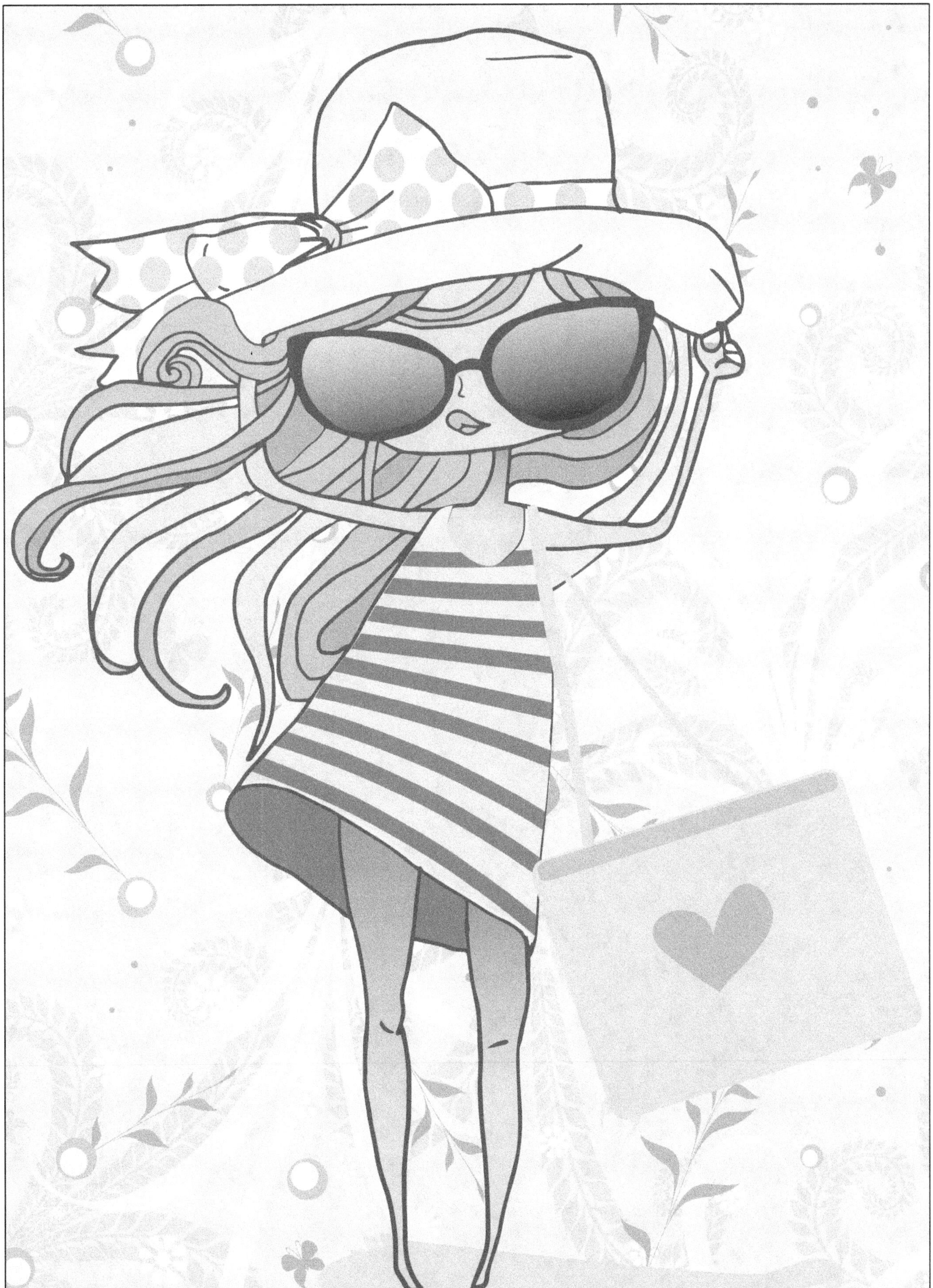

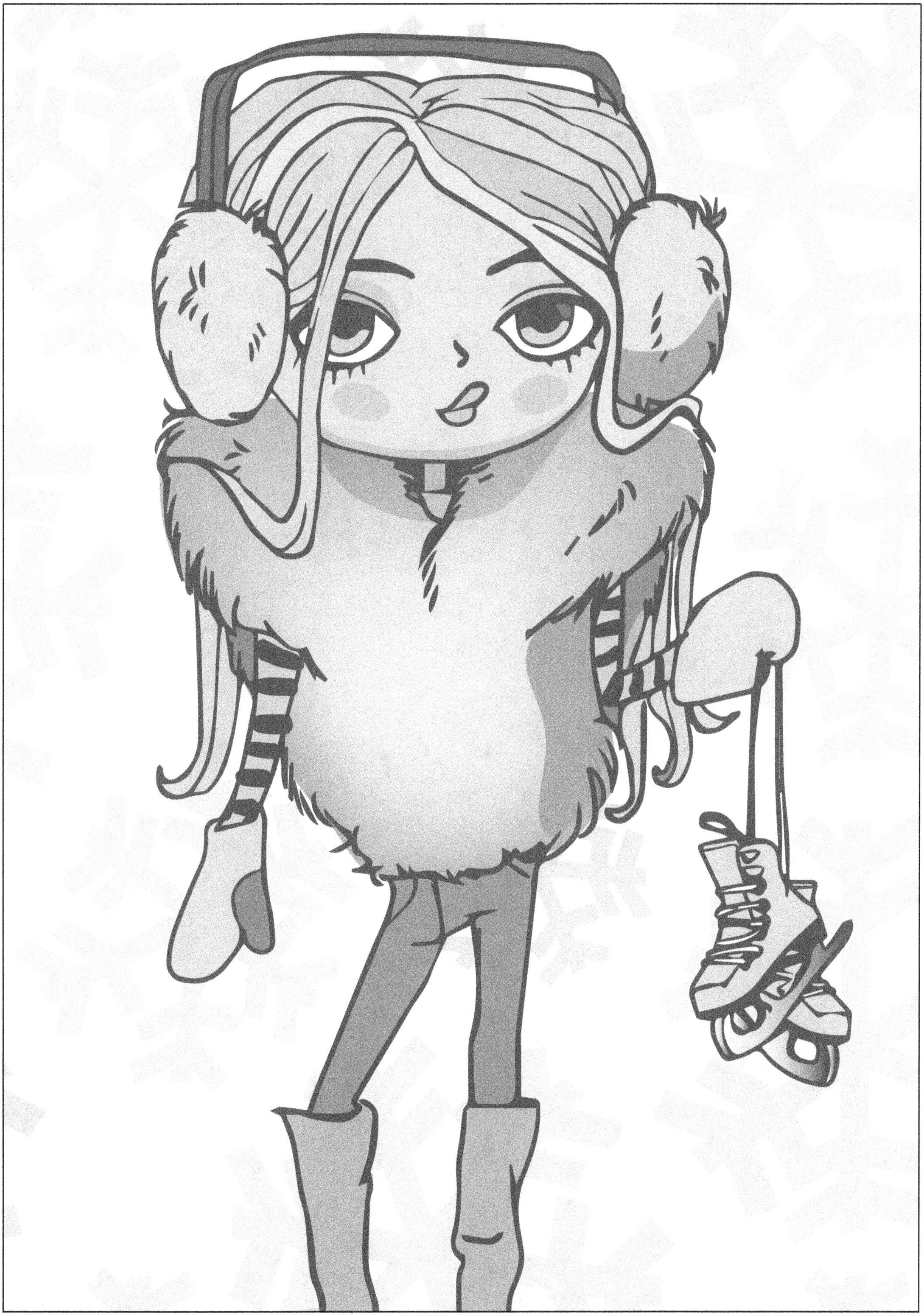

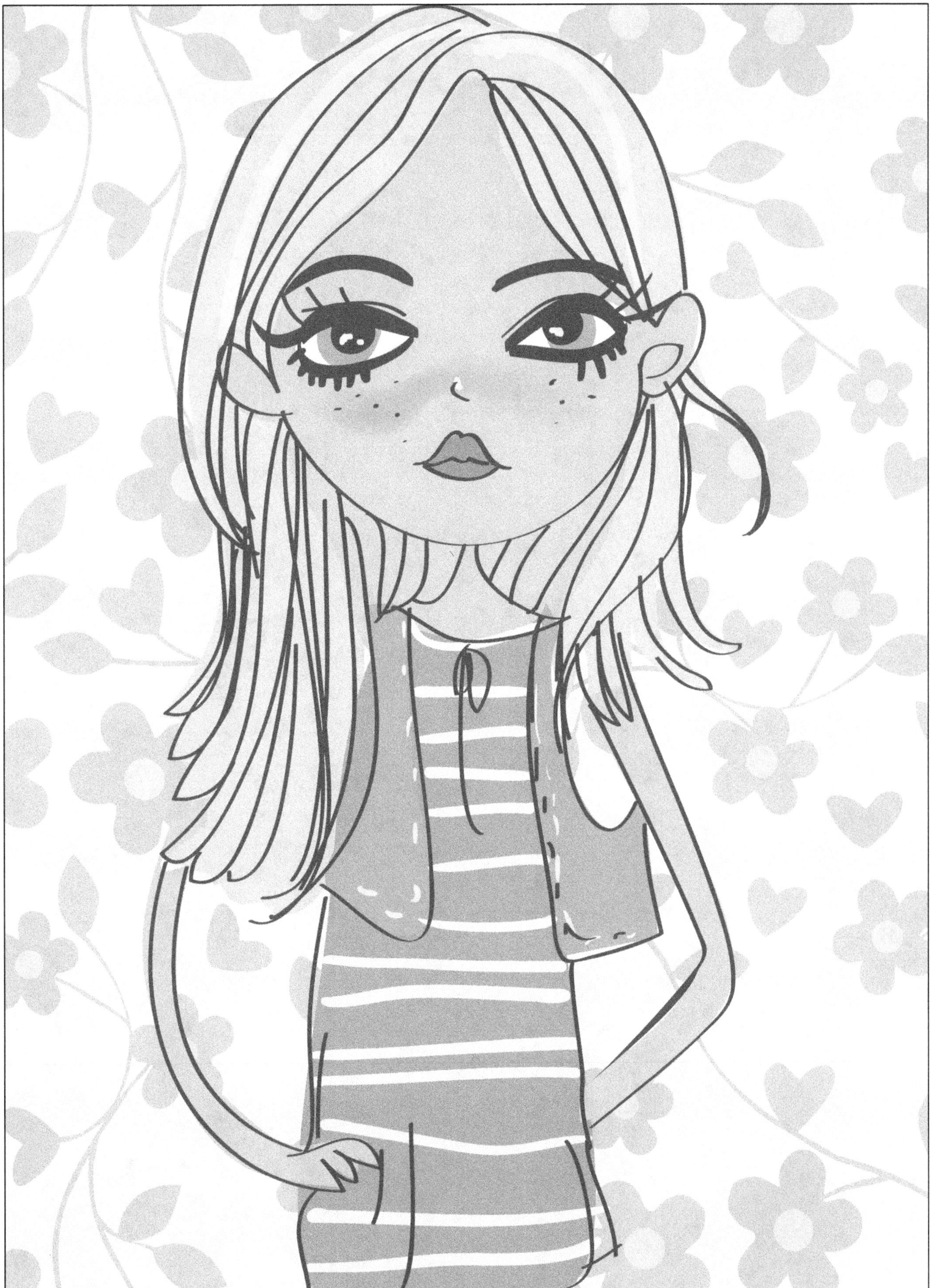

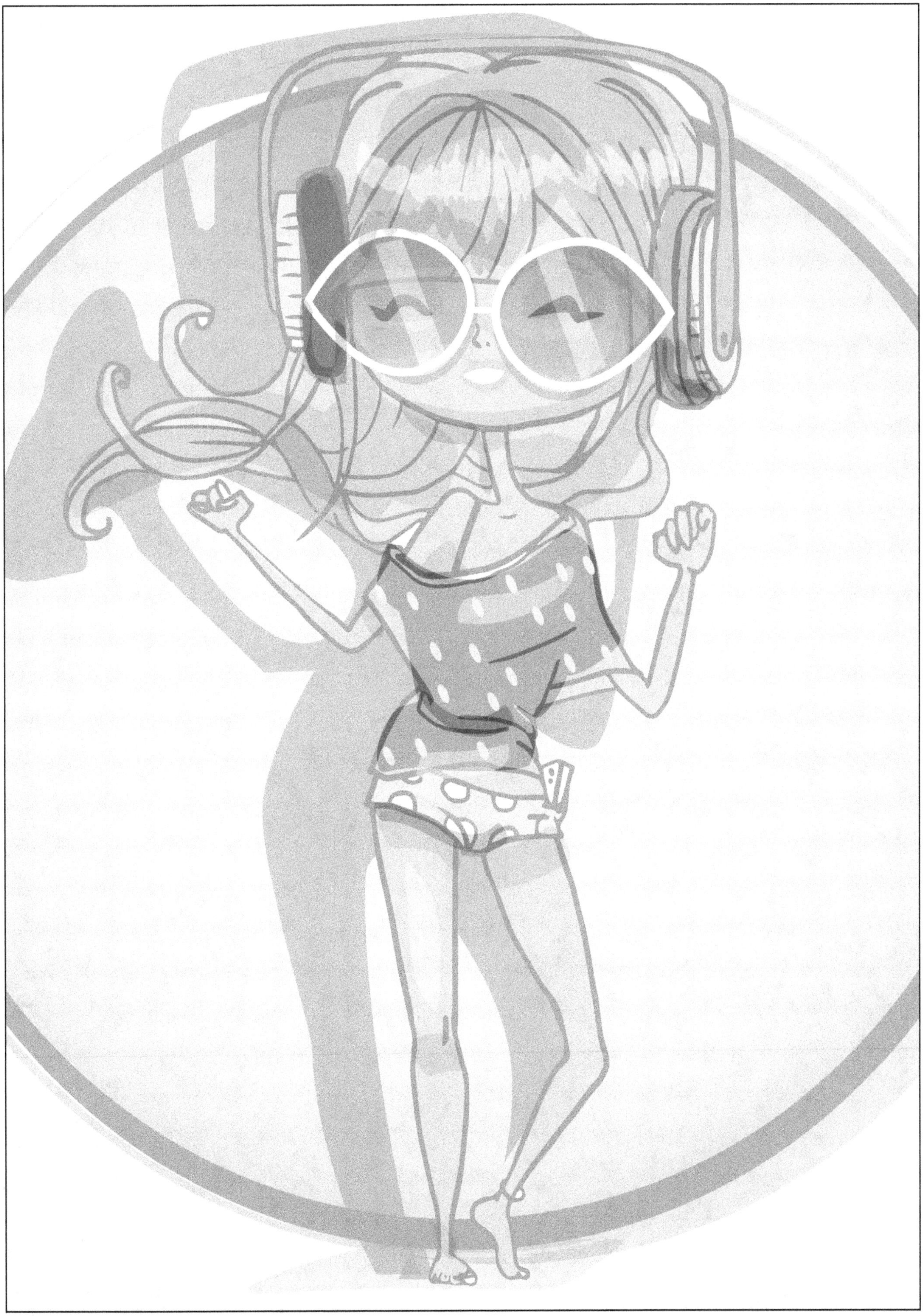

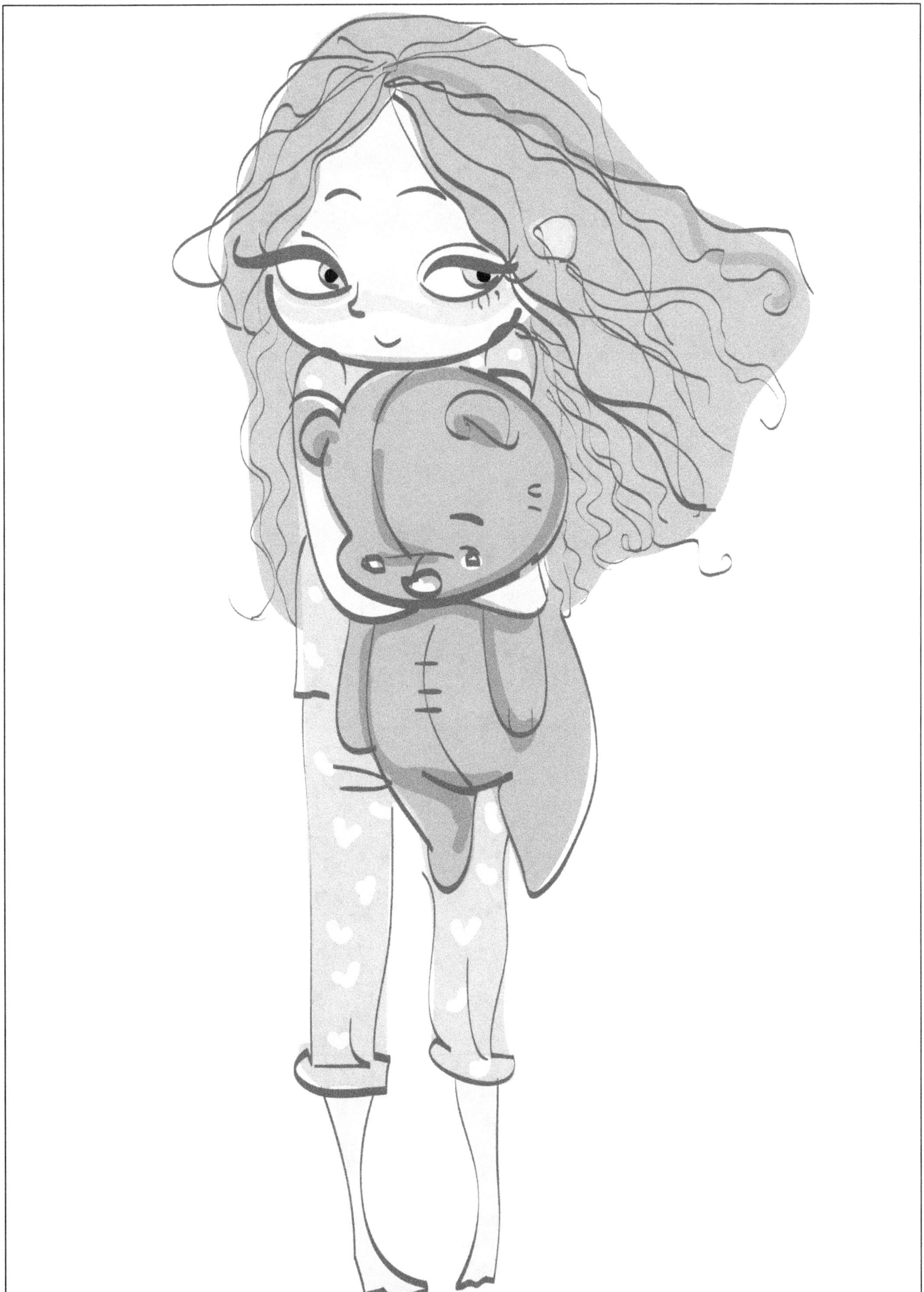

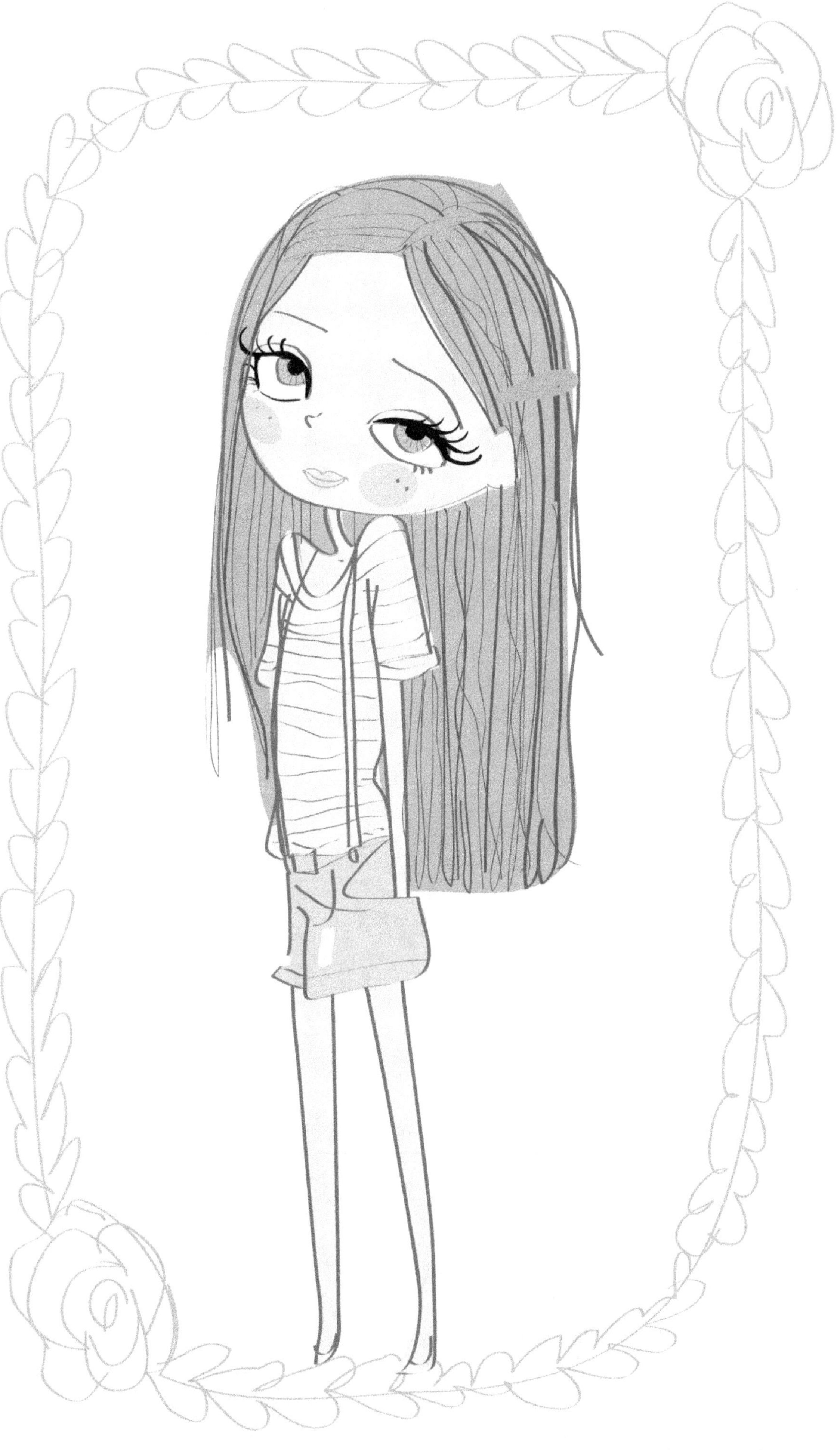

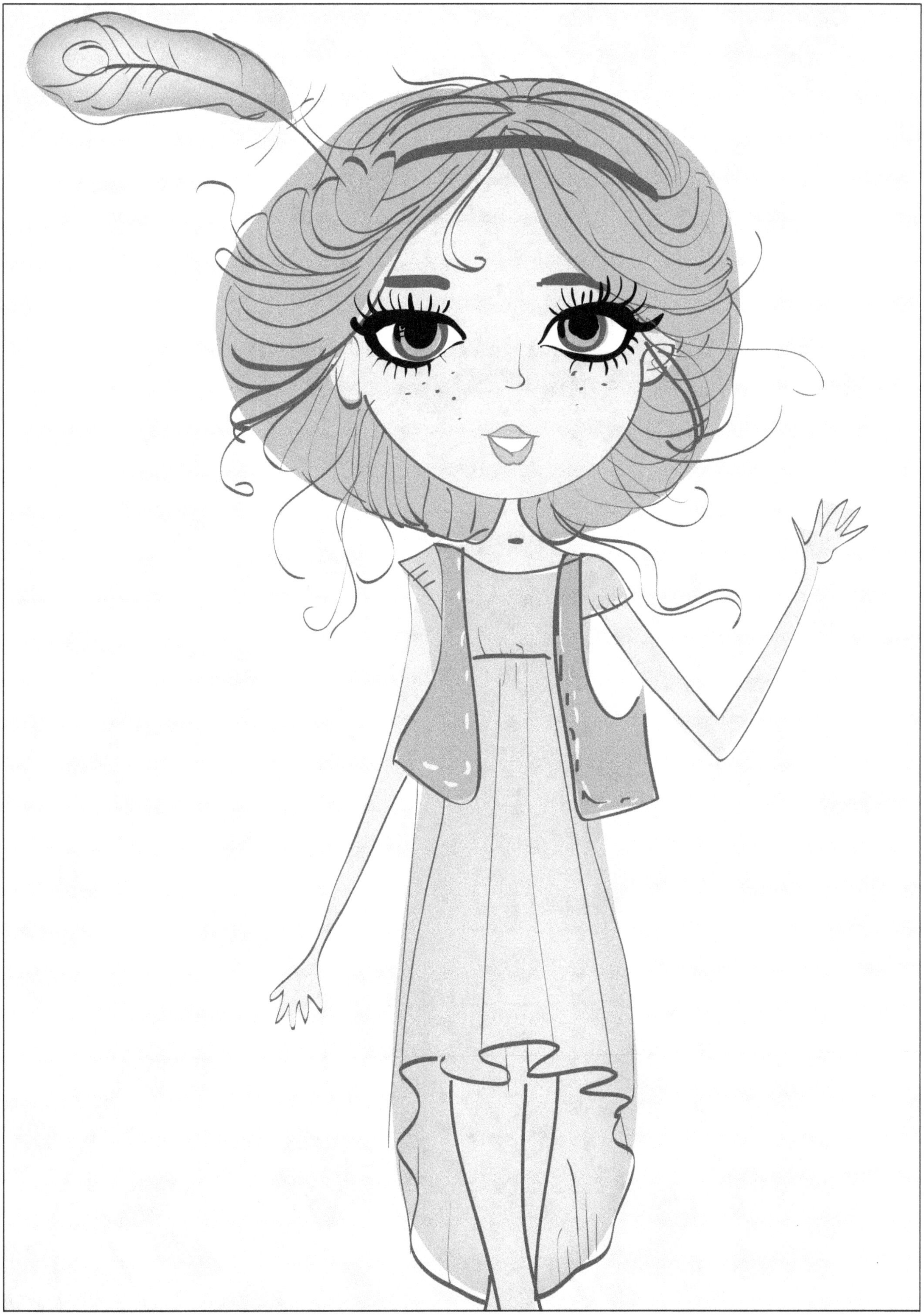

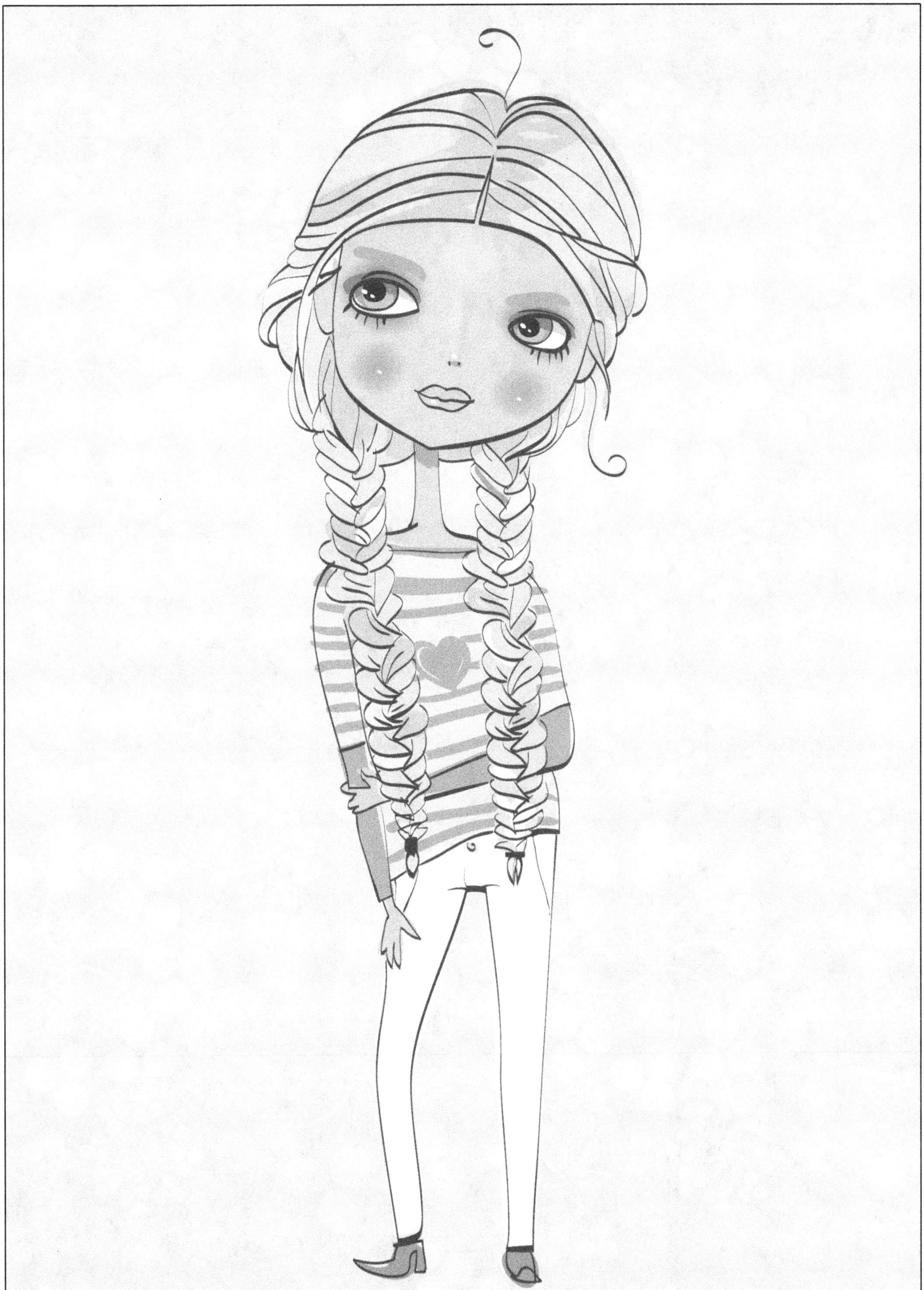

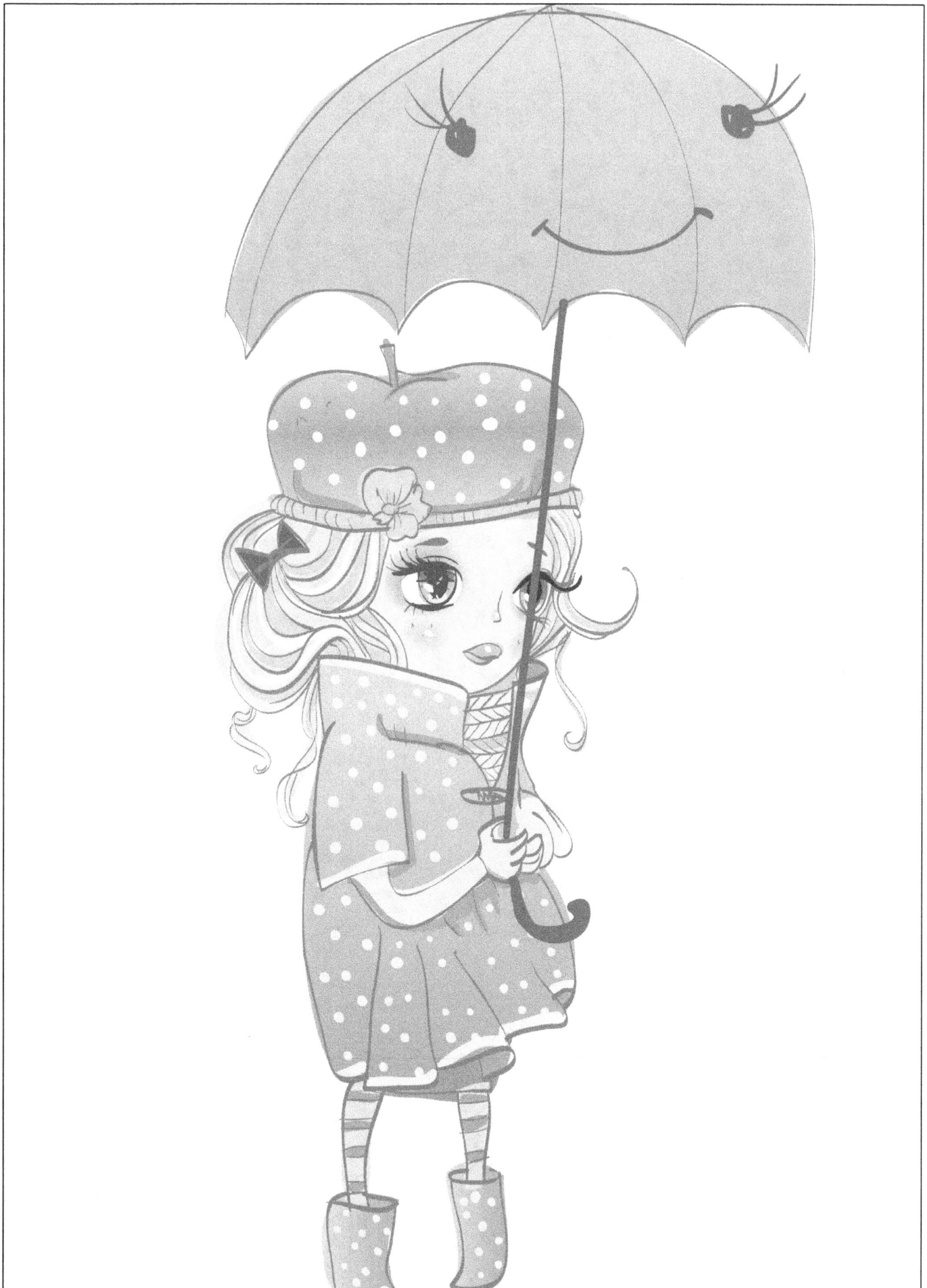

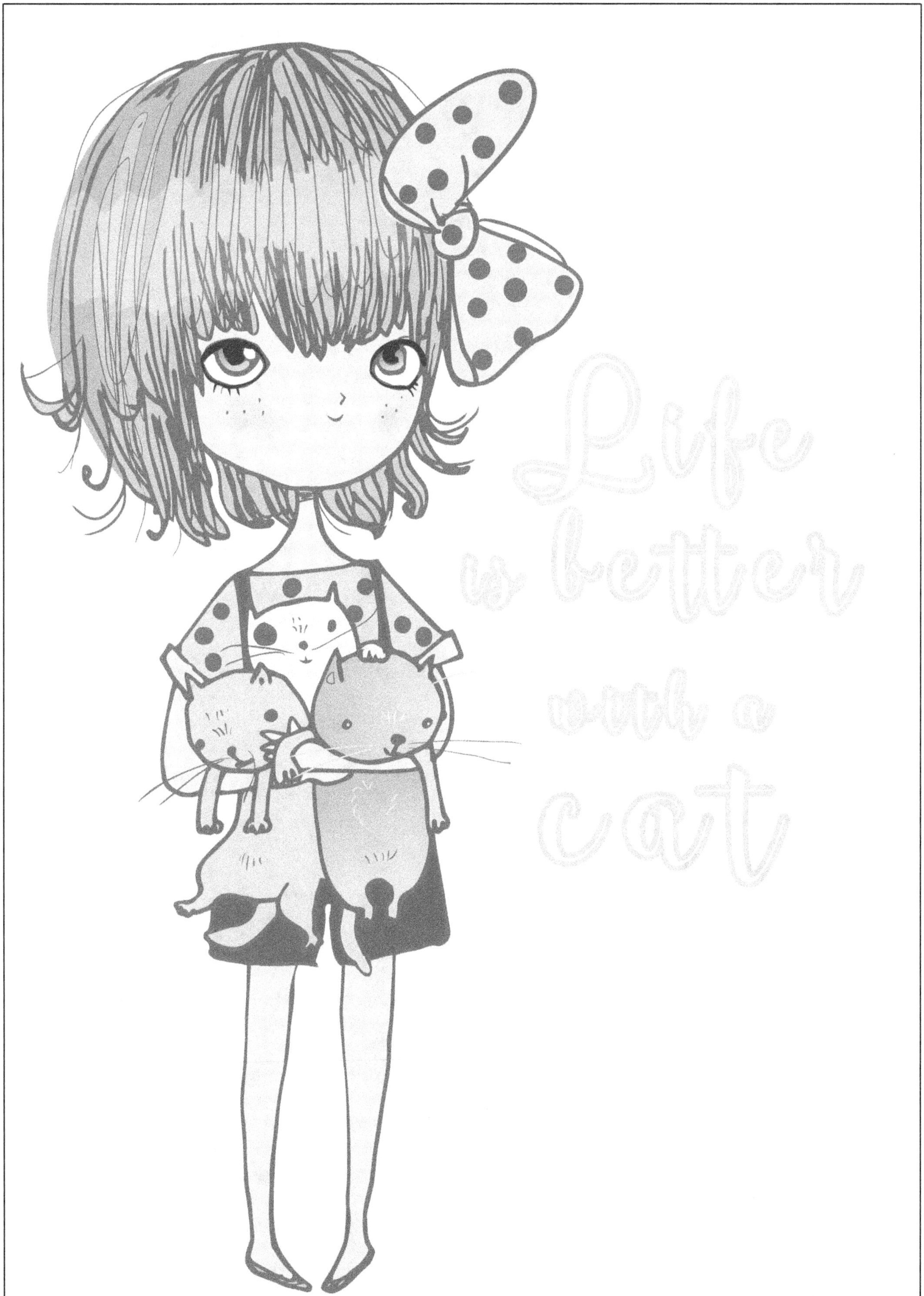
Life
is better
with a
cat

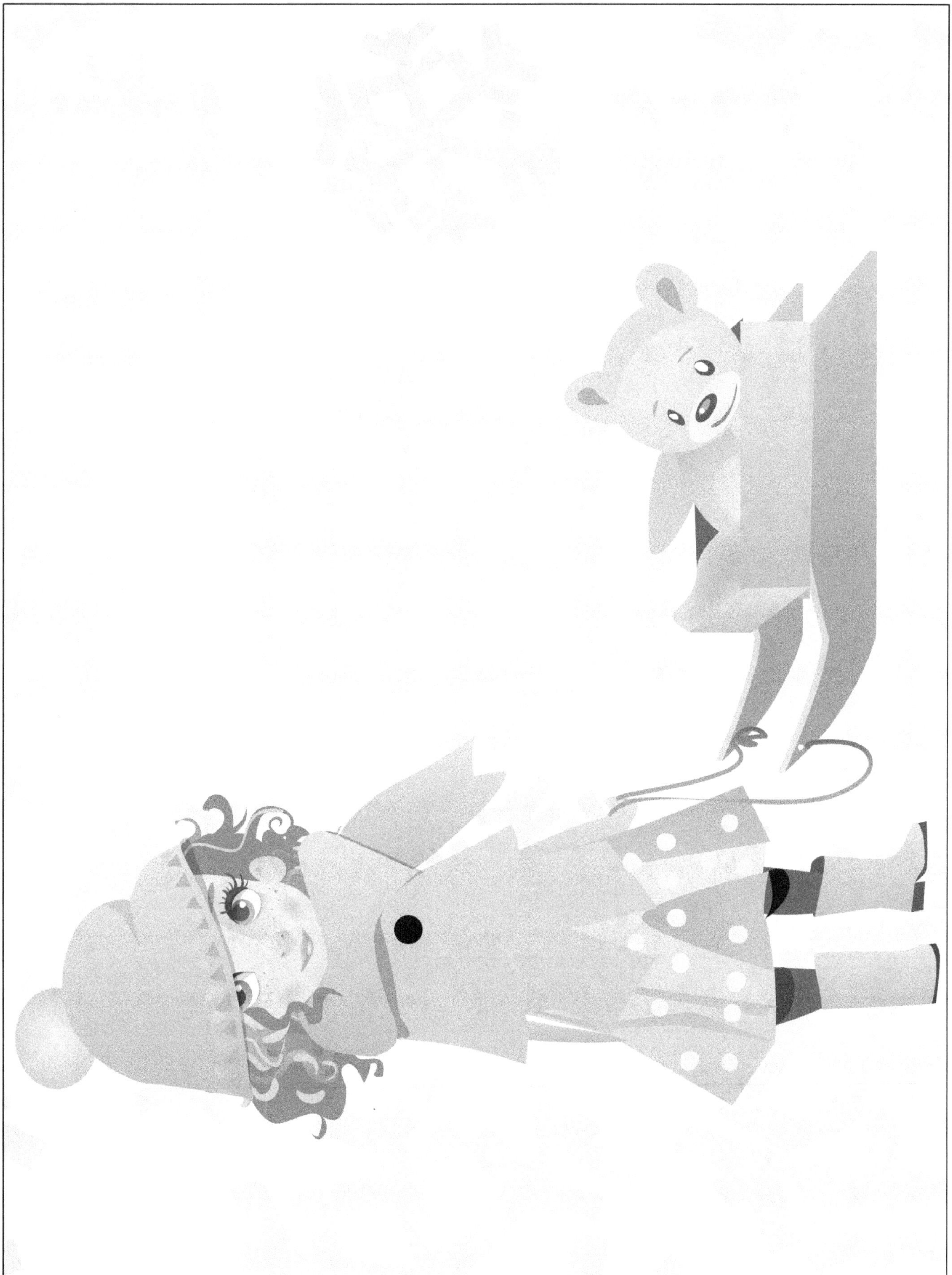

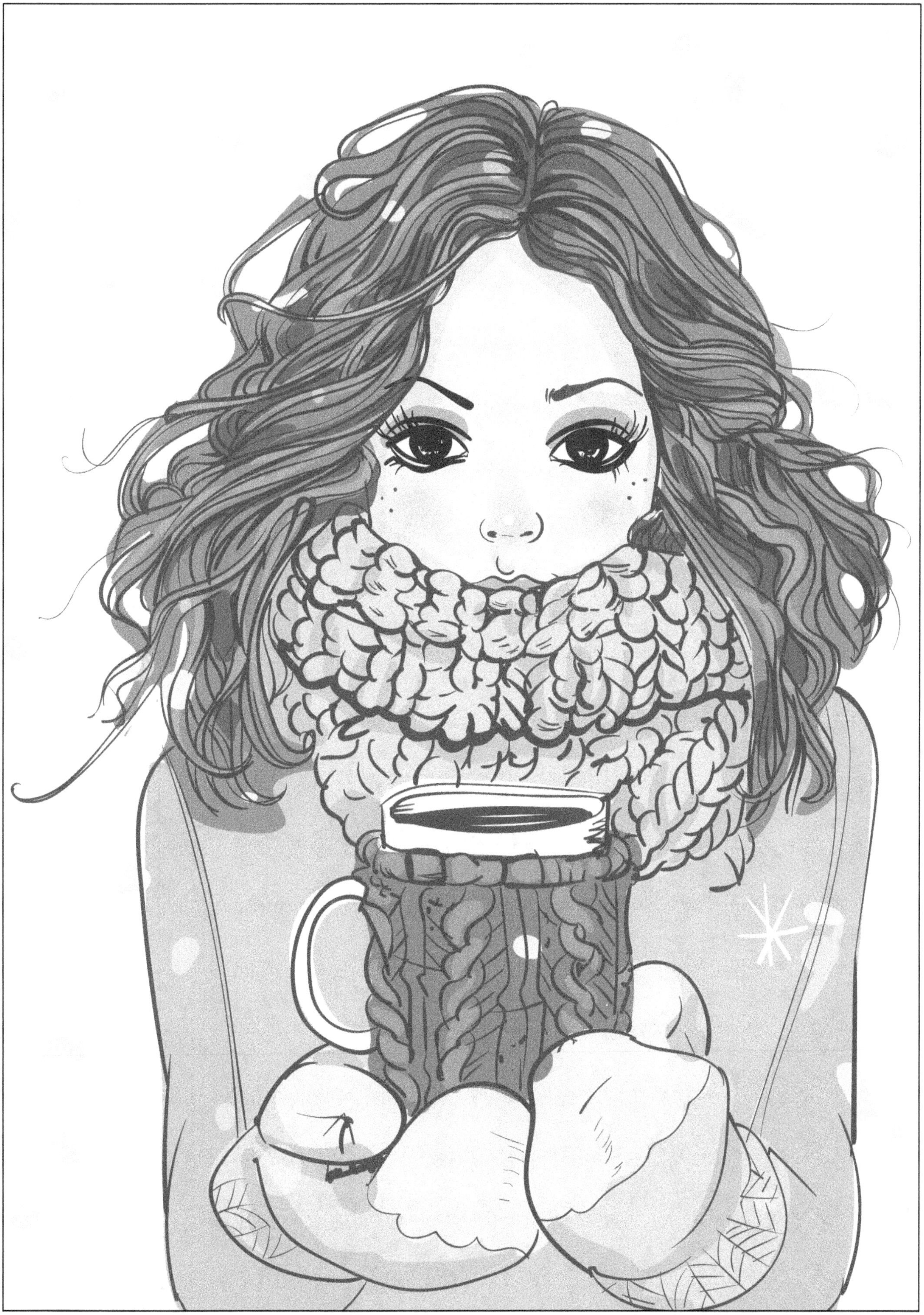

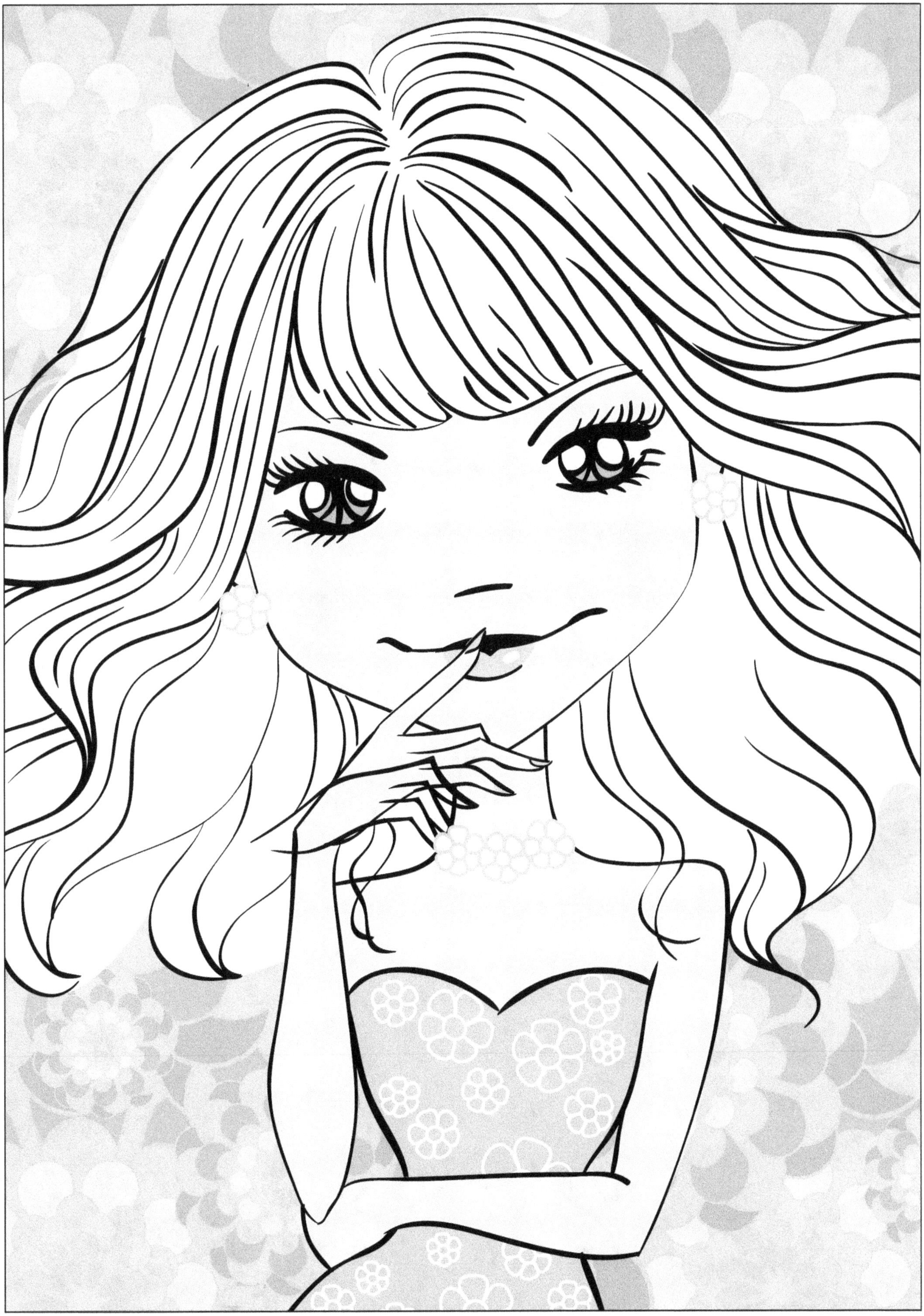

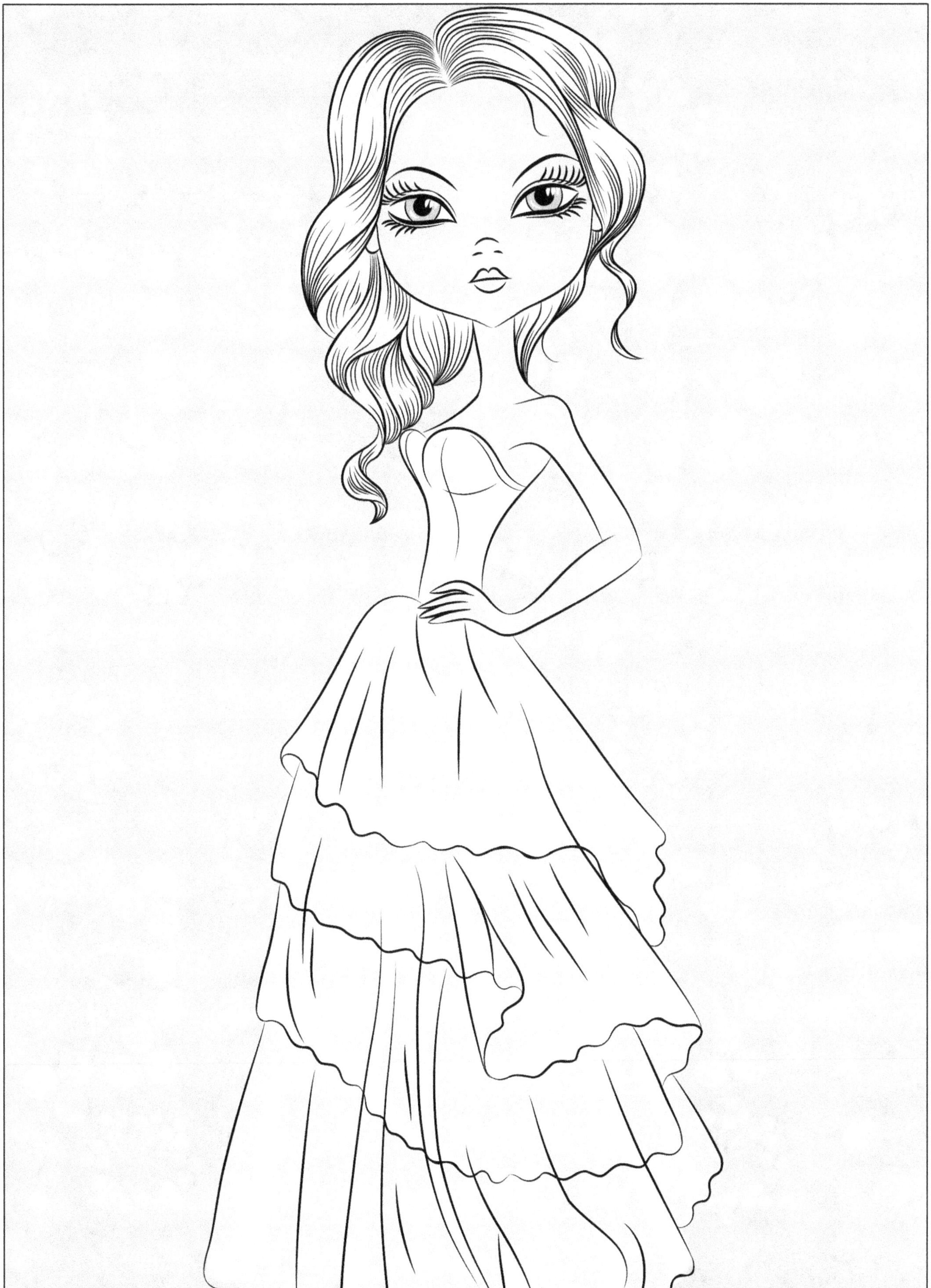

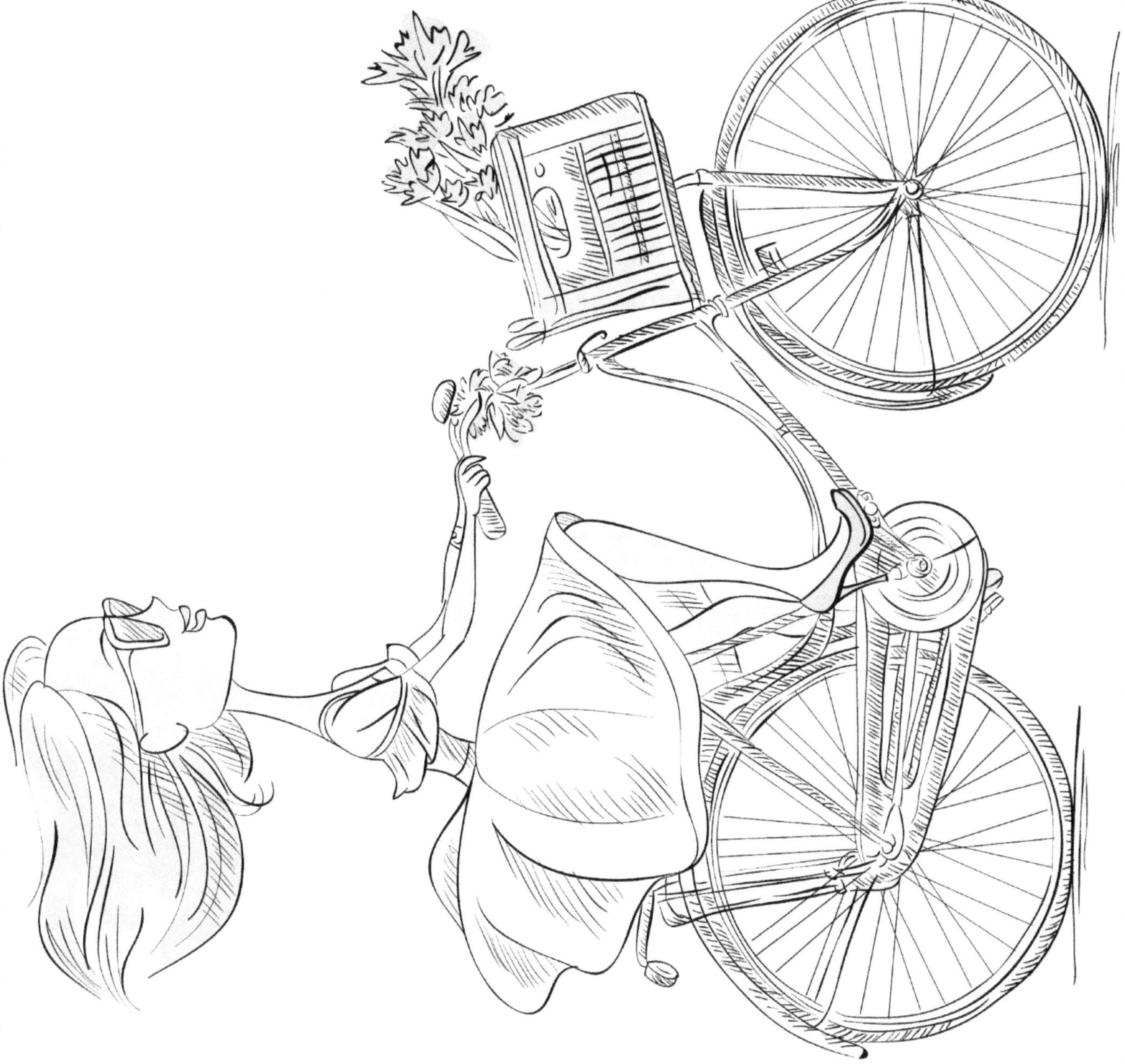

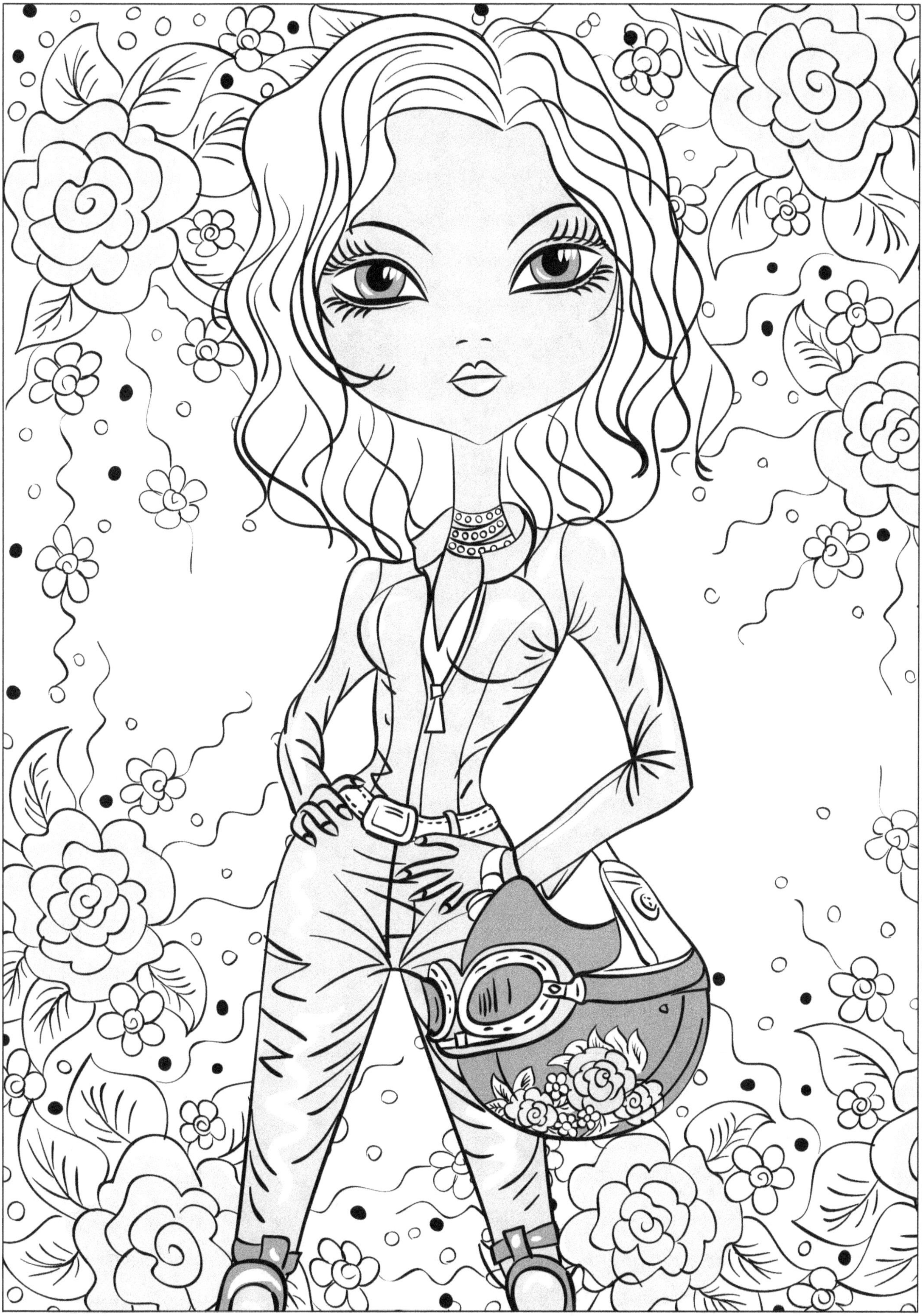

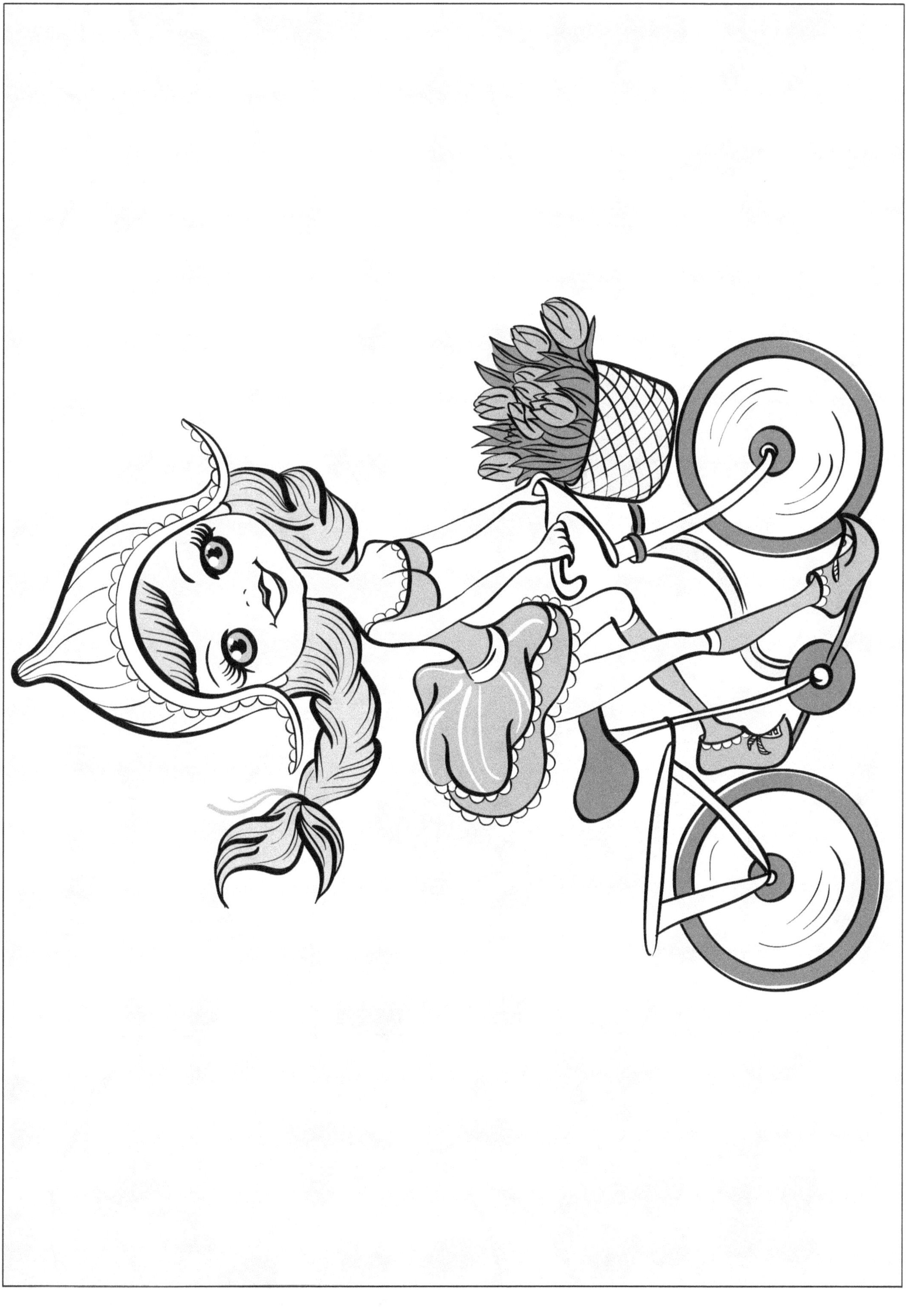

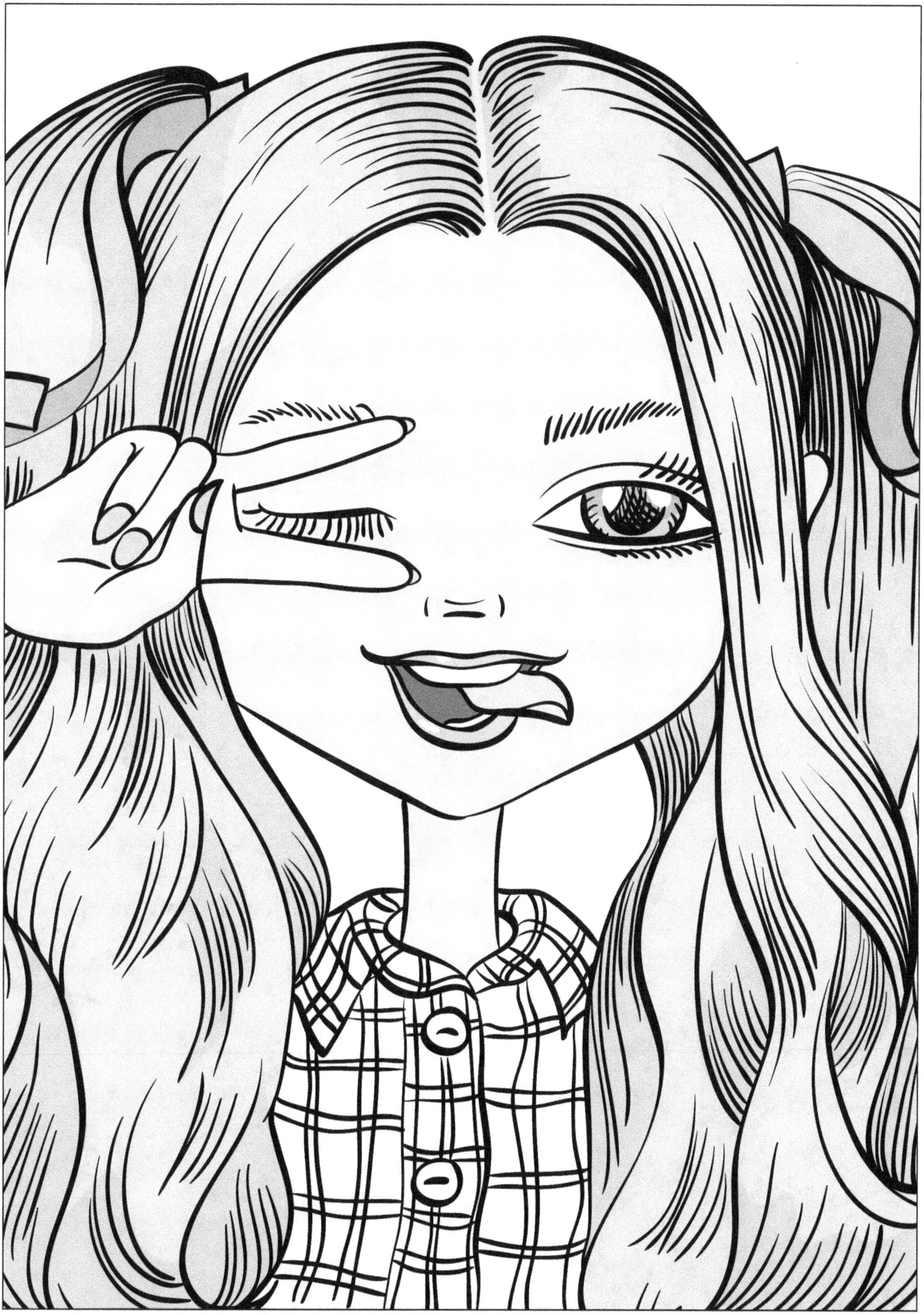

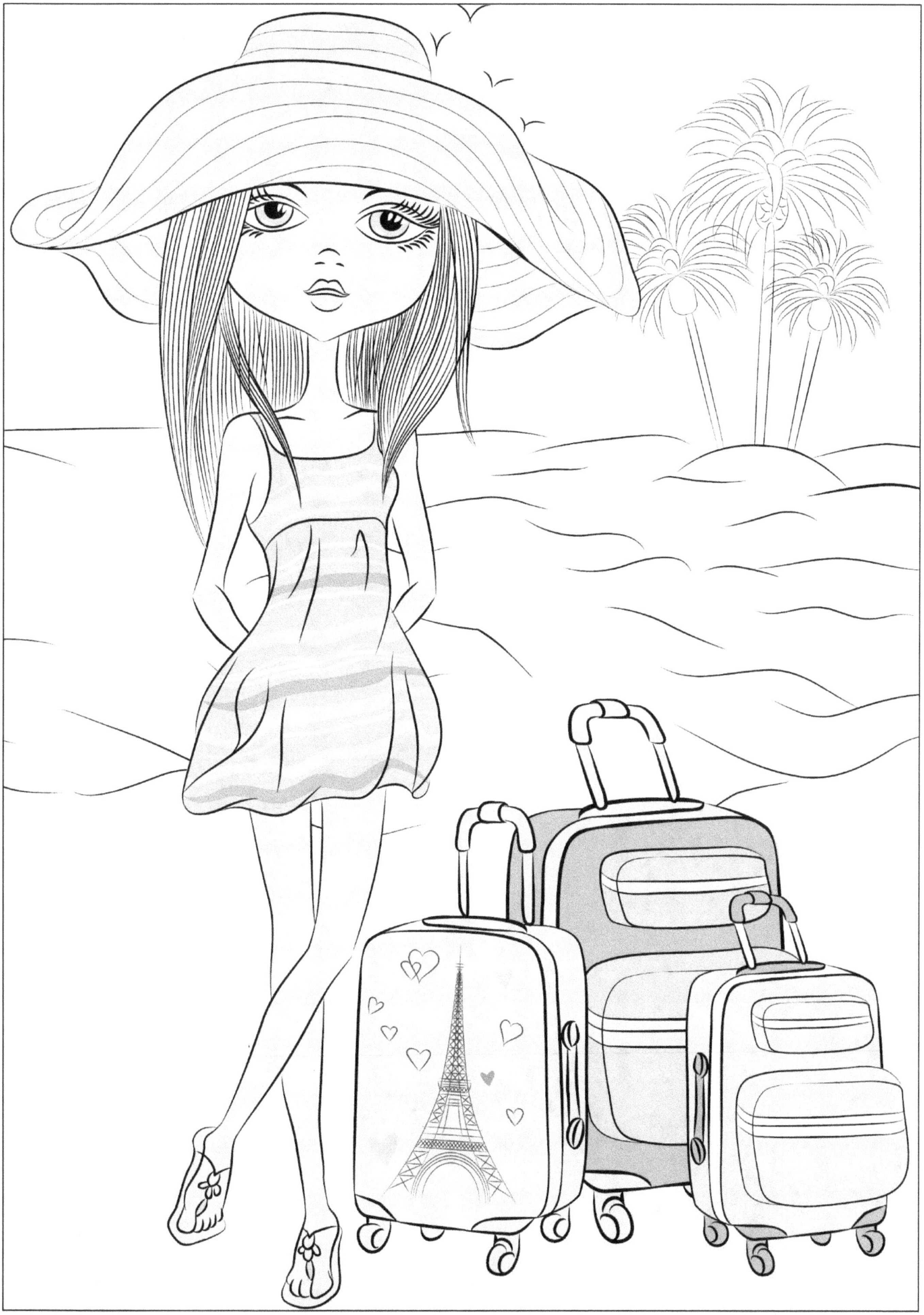

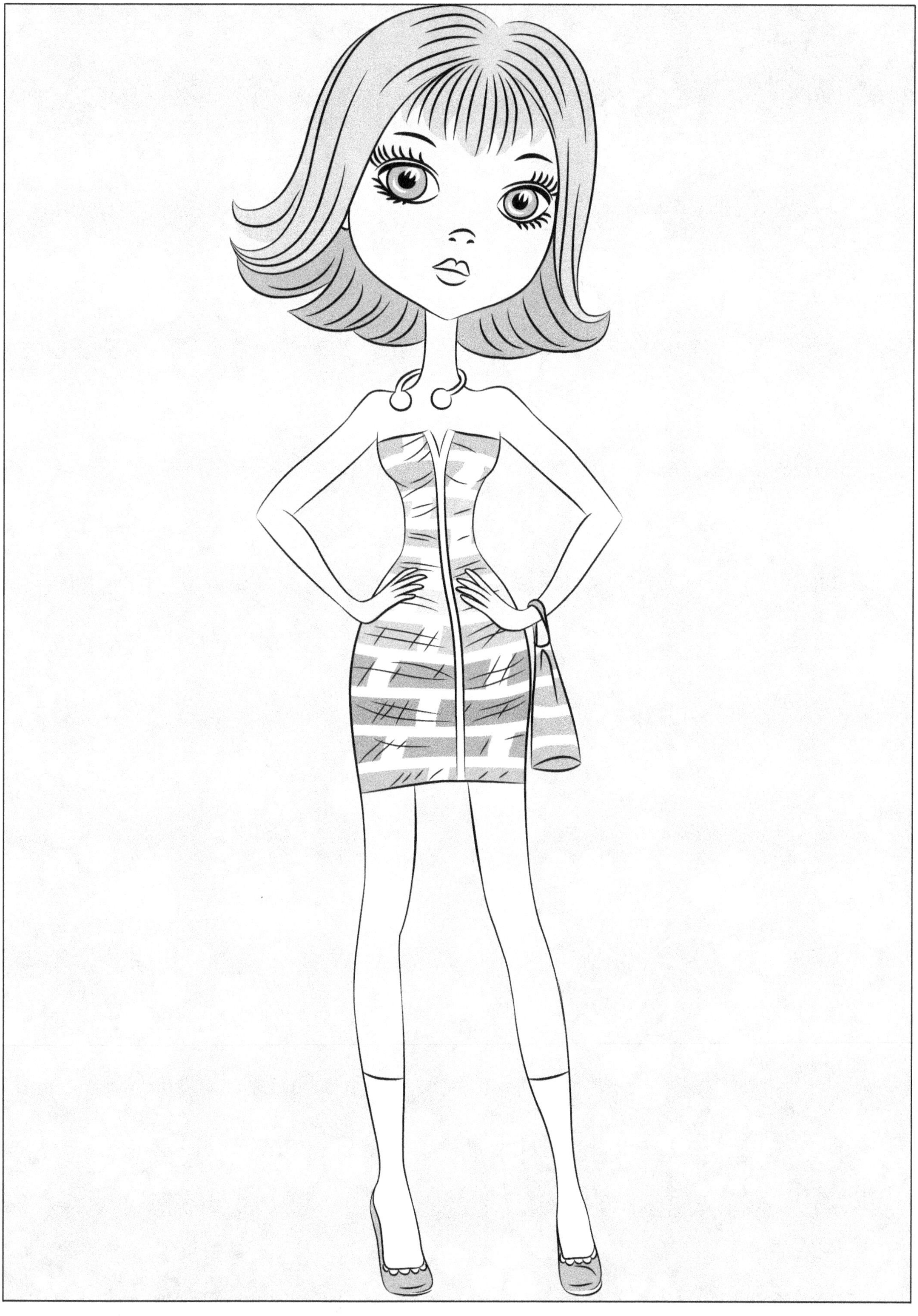

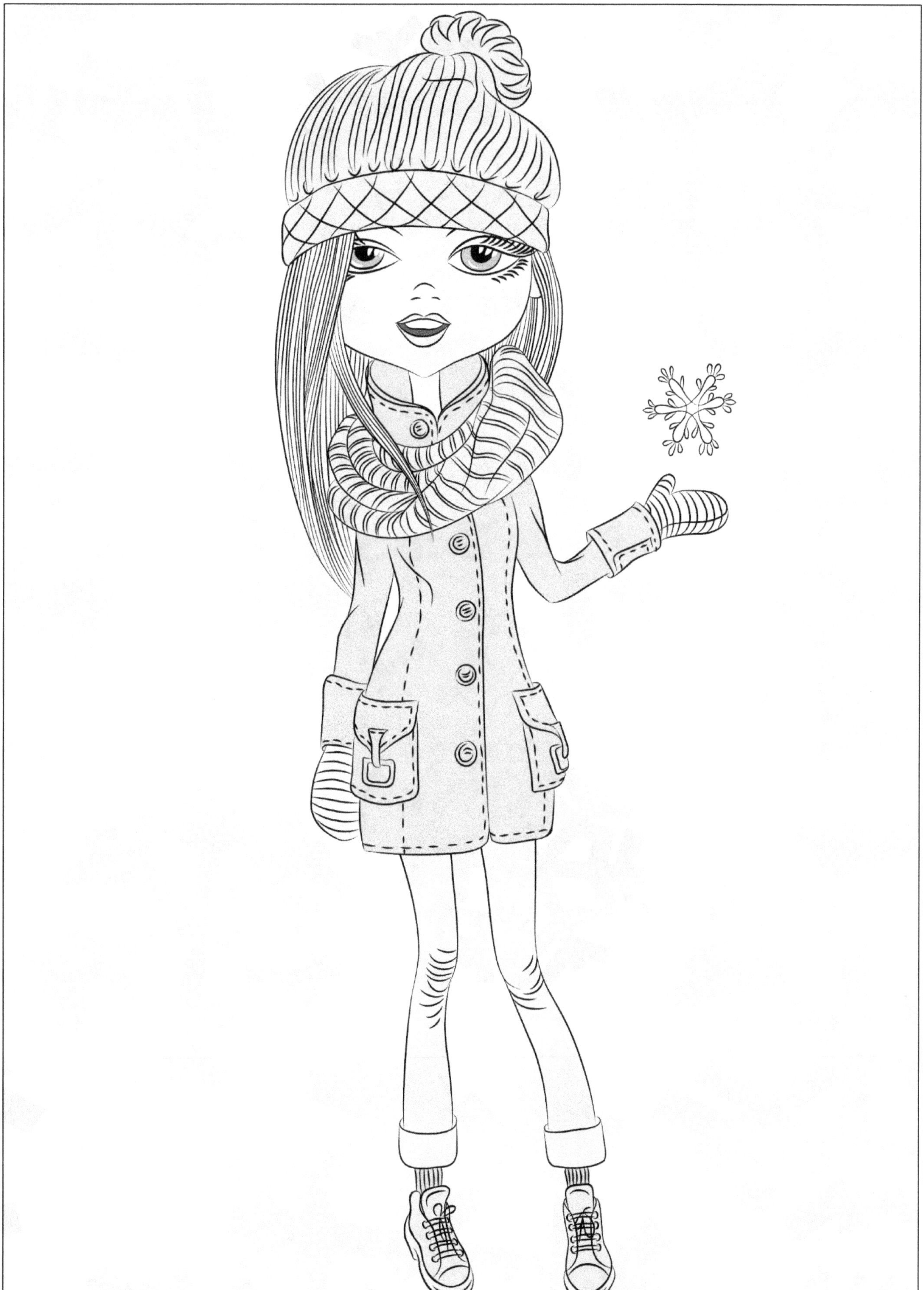

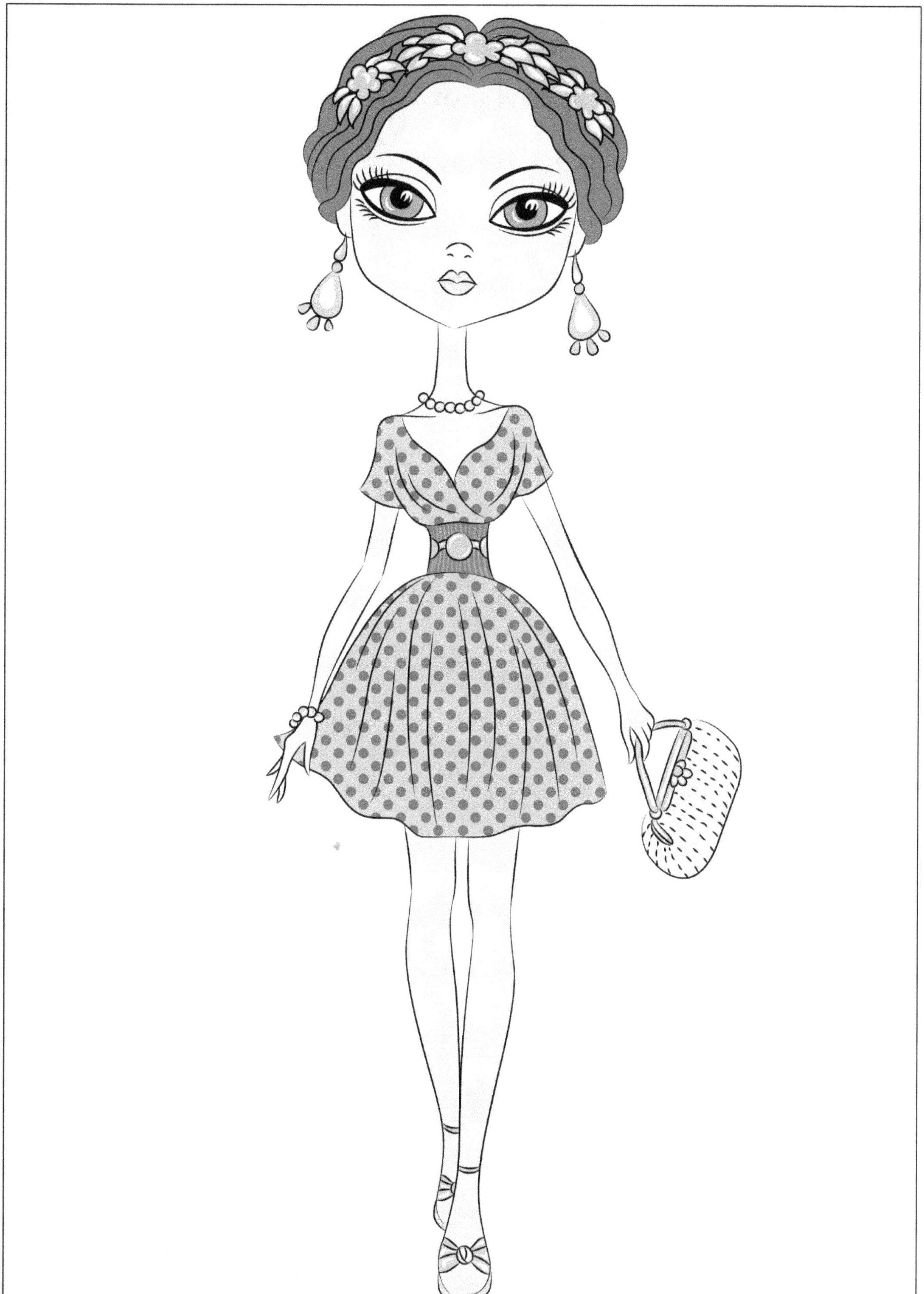

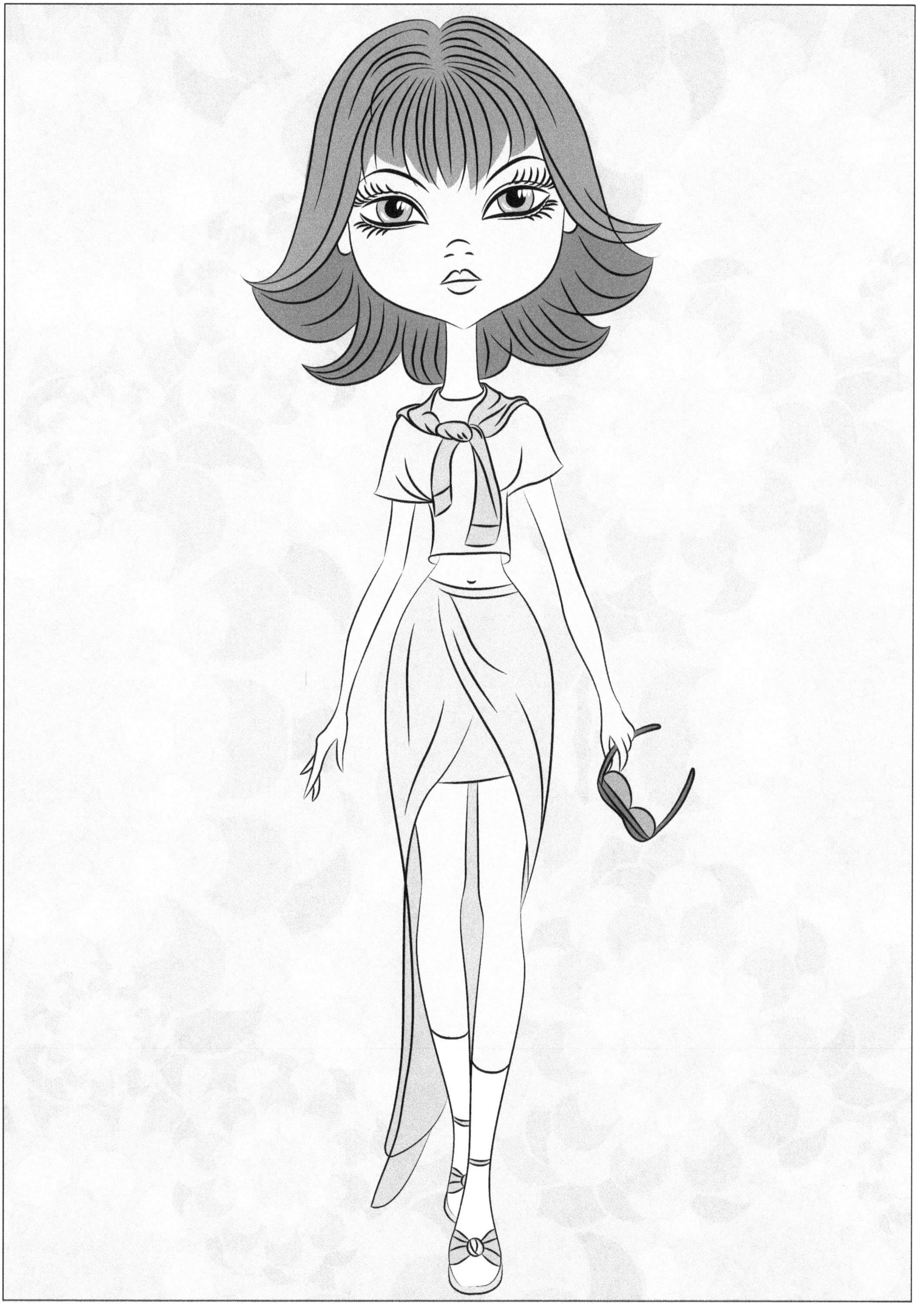

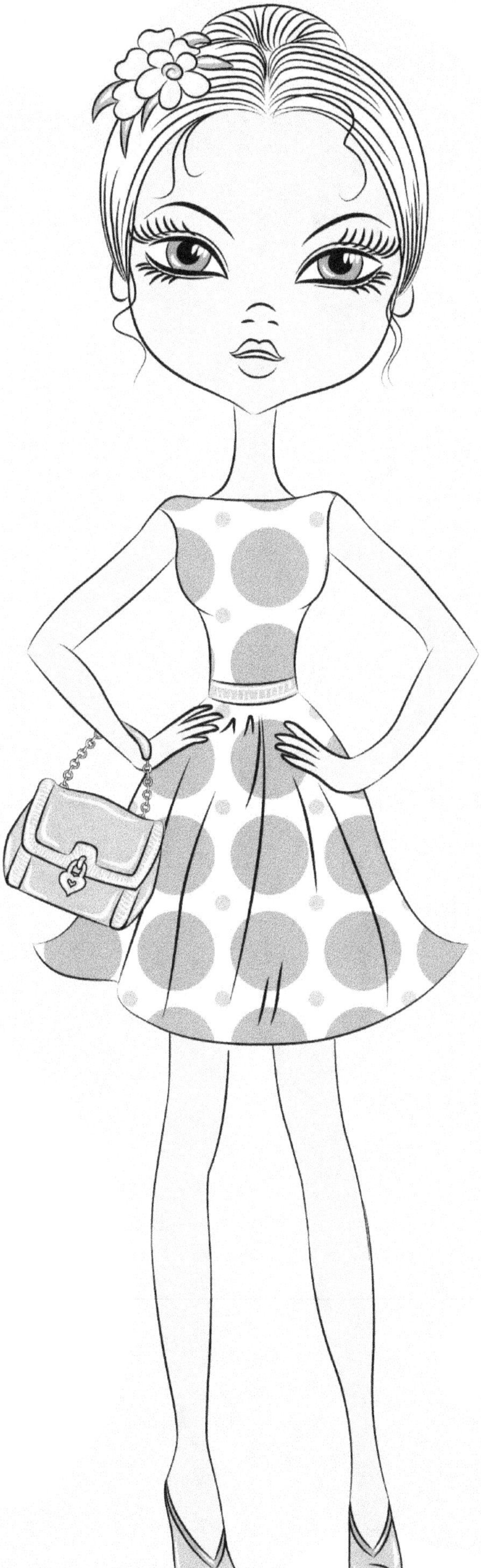

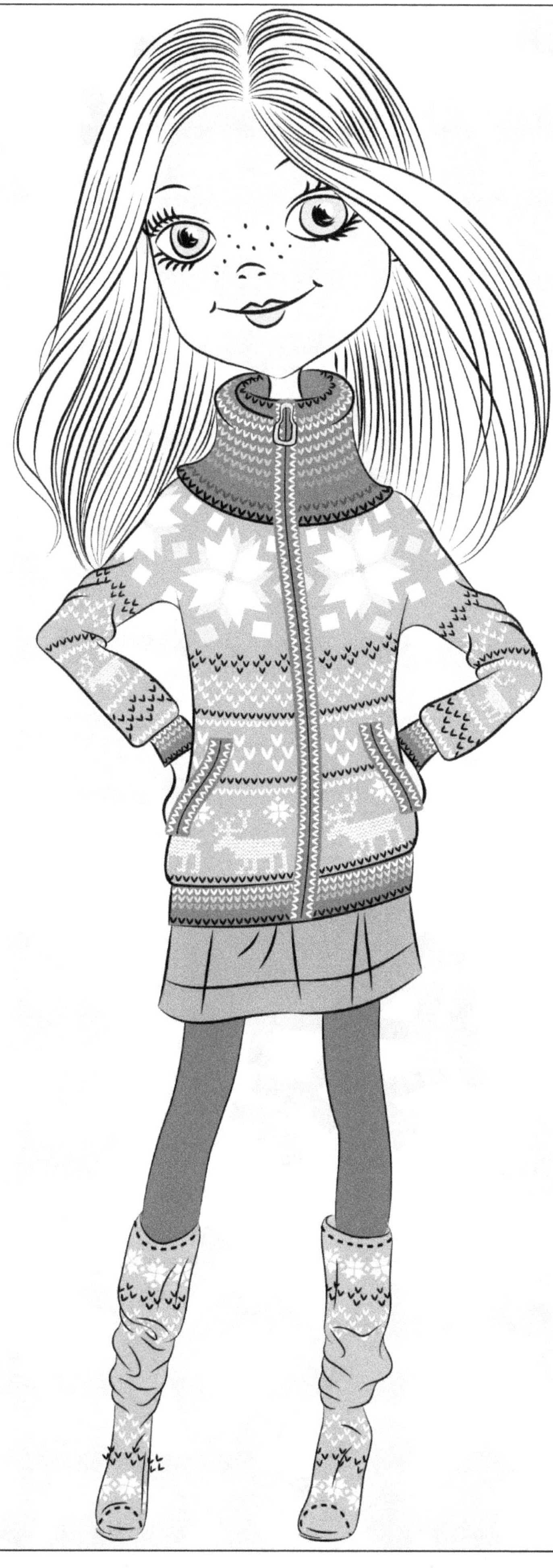

www.ingramcontent.com/pod-product-compliance
Lightning Source LLC
Chambersburg PA
CBHW081304170526
45165CB00011B/3405